# Language and Literacy in the Early Years Foundation Stage

Children's early communication needs careful nurturing and support. Practitioners will be both challenged and supported by this book which focuses on the skills needed for language and literacy and all aspects of children's interaction with others.

The learning opportunities for children need to be relevant for their age group, realistic and challenging. This book gives readers clear explanations and practical ideas to help them establish firm foundations on which children can grow in confidence and become skilful communicators.

**Helen Bradford** is a senior Early Years tutor at the Faculty of Education, University of Cambridge. She has a teaching background in nursery education and has written extensively for *Nursery World* magazine.

**Practical Guidance in the EYFS**
Series Editor: Sandy Green

The *Practical Guidance in the EYFS* series will assist practitioners in the smooth and successful implementation of the Early Years Foundation Stage.

Each book gives clear and detailed explanations of each aspect of learning and development and encourages readers to consider each area within its broadest context to expand and develop their own knowledge and good practice.

Practical ideas and activities for all age groups are offered along with a wealth of expertise of how elements from the practice guidance can be implemented within all early years' settings. The books include suggestions for the innovative use of everyday resources, popular books and stories.

Titles in this series include:

# Communication, Language and Literacy in the Early Years Foundation Stage

Helen Bradford

Routledge
Taylor & Francis Group

LONDON AND NEW YORK

First published 2009
by Routledge
2 Park Square, Milton Park, Abingdon, Oxon OX14 4RN

Simultaneously published in the USA and Canada
by Routledge
270 Madison Avenue, New York, NY 10016

*Routledge is an imprint of the Taylor and Francis Group, an informa business*

© 2009 Helen Shelbourne (publishing under the name Helen Bradford)

Typeset in Optima by
Taylor & Francis Books
Printed and bound in Great Britain by
TJ International Ltd, Padstow, Cornwall

*British Library Cataloguing in Publication Data*
A catalogue record for this book is available from the British Library

*Library of Congress Cataloging in Publication Data*
Bradford, Helen.
 Communication, language, and literacy in the early years foundation stage /
 Helen Bradford.
   p. cm. – (Practical guidance in the EYFS)
 Includes bibliographical references. 1. Children–Language. 2. Language
 arts (Early childhood) 3. Child development. I. Title.
 LB1139.L3B675 2009
 372.6–dc22                                      2008026668

ISBN 978-0-415-47835-9 (hbk)
ISBN 978-0-415-47427-6 (pbk)

For Ed

# Contents

# Acknowledgements

Many thanks to my colleague Dominic Wyse for his input. An extremely useful resource to have in your setting for parents and carers to borrow, or to recommend, is Dominic's book *How to Help Your Child Read and Write*, Harlow: Pearson Prentice Hall Life (2007).

# Introduction

> Every child deserves the best possible start in life and support to fulfil their potential. A child's experience in the early years has a major impact on their future life chances.
>
> (Department for Education and Skills [DfES] 2007a: 7)

Early years providers have a duty to ensure that their early years provision complies with learning and development requirements as set out in the Statutory Framework for the Early Years Foundation Stage (EYFS) (DfES 2007a). Set against a background of new legislation, the aim of the EYFS framework (DfES 2007a) is to support young children to achieve the five Every Child Matters (ECM) (DfES 2003) outcomes of staying safe, being healthy, enjoying and achieving, making a positive contribution, and achieving economic well-being. In addition, effective early years practice must be built on the four overall guiding themes of a unique child, positive relationships, enabling environments, and learning and development; themes that provide a context for the requirements of the EYFS framework (DfES 2007a) and that state how practitioners can support the development, learning and care of young children. Alongside the EYFS framework (DfES 2007a), information and advice has been provided by the DfES in the form of the *Practice Guidance for the EYFS* (DfES 2007b) which sets out six interrelated areas of learning and development. This book will support practitioners on both a theoretical and practical level in relation to the area of learning and development entitled communication, language and literacy. It is designed to give background and ideas to effectively facilitate the development of children's learning and competence in communicating through speaking and listening, reading and writing. Such development of children's learning thrives in an ethos where they are encouraged and supported as shown in Figure 1.

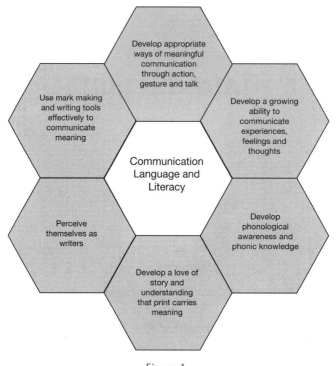

*Figure 1*
What Communication, Language and Literacy mean for children
Source: DfES 2007b

The book will be an invaluable resource for all those who work with young children, providing:

- theoretical frameworks in which to challenge early years practitioners to reflect on their own practice and attitudes; and
- additional ideas and activities for developing and extending the suggestions made for effective practice to support the practical implementation of the EYFS framework (2007a), making links to early learning goals as appropriate and including ideas for relevant books and resources.

The book uses the main headings from the practice guidance for the EYFS (DfES 2007b) and keeps as close as possible to its format. The activities include key questions and are closely linked to the EYFS curriculum so that learning outcomes can be easily monitored and evaluated. The book follows the series format which includes a summary of relevant theories at the beginning. The chapter headings follow the sections of learning and development as set out in the *Practice Guidance for the EYFS* (DfES 2007b) (see Figure 2).

Each chapter relates to the full age range and incorporates the early learning goals as shown in Figure 3.

Key words are highlighted from the practice-guidance element and early learning goals relating to each separate age range under discussion in every chapter.

Each developmental aspect has one main story allocated across the age range, taking into account the fact that children will not follow a linear pattern of development. Practitioners are also given a range of alternative titles to choose from, as it is important that they feel comfortable with and enthusiastic about the texts they use with their children. Each story provides the basis for a number of activities and a list of additional resources is included which can be used in relation to these. Activities are closely related to the other three categories in the learning and development sections in the practice guidance for the EYFS (DfES 2007b) where practitioners must

*Figure 2*
Sections of learning and development for communication, language and literacy
Source: DfES 2007b

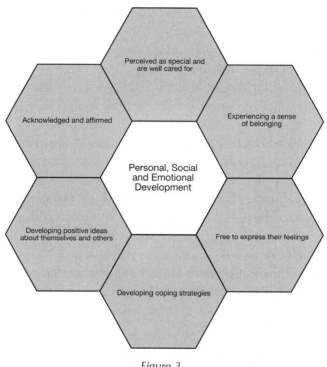

*Figure 3*
The age range for the EYFS
Source: DfES 2007b

look, listen and note, be effective in their practice and scrutinise the appropriateness of their planning and resourcing. Essentially, each chapter builds on established good practice, supporting practitioners in extending their children's communication, language and literacy ability.

# A theoretical basis

## .1 Language for communication and thinking: language acquisition and the development of speaking and listening skills

### Language acquisition

By the age of five, provided they do not have language difficulties, all children have acquired the adult grammar for the main constructions of their

native language (Peccei 2006). This is true across all cultures
languages. The term 'acquired' in this context is important becaus
make a distinction between emergent language constructions
which are fully acquired. Nature versus nurture arguments are stil
debated in relation to how children's language develops. One of the most
famous advocates of the idea that language development is natural was
Noam Chomsky. In his early work he hypothesised that children make use
of a language acquisition device (LAD), a special capacity of the brain that
enables them to use the rules systems of their native language. Jerome
Bruner argued that Chomsky's theory correctly identified this aspect of the
child's capacity but that this was only part of the process of language
acquisition. Bruner acknowledged a clear role for adults as experienced
language users in relation to children's language acquisition;

> The infant's Language Acquisition Device could not function with-
> out the aid given by an adult who enters with him into a transac-
> tional format. That format, initially under the control of the adult,
> provides a Language Acquisition Support System (LASS). It frames
> or structures the input of language and interaction to the child's
> Language Acquisition Device in a manner to 'make the system func-
> tion.' In a word, it is the interaction between the LAD and the LASS
> that makes it possible for the infant to enter the linguistic commu-
> nity – and, at the same time, the culture to which the language
> gives access.
>
> (Bruner 1983: 19)

Messer (2006) shows the ways that such debates have continued to be an
important part of thinking about children's language acquisition. Chomsky's
later work involved theories of minimalism. One of the important features of
minimalist theory is the idea that many aspects of grammar are contained in
the vocabulary of a language, and its semantic information (meaning).
Previous theories proposed that grammatical representations were independent of the vocabulary. Minimalist ideas and other developments in the field
have resulted in language development theorists focusing on the way that
the human brain operates more generally. Neuroscientists have defined the
brain's activity in terms of connectionist networks, neural networks or par-
allel distributed processes, which are terms describing the same phenom-
ena. The point of such work is to research the extent to which language
features are innate or can be learned.

A resurgence of interest in how adults speak to children must also be considered. One of the important ideas in relation to children's language acquisition has been the concept of motherese, the impact, appropriateness and helpfulness of language interactions, particularly between mothers and their children (see Tizard and Hughes, 1984). This is now called child-directed speech (CDS) in recognition of the fact that it is not just mothers who modify their speech when talking to young children but many key adults involved in a child's life. Peccei (2006) points out that there is no clear evidence that CDS should be seen particularly as a teaching tool. She accurately observes that CDS is probably just a natural response to the fact that young children use talk which is semantically and syntactically simple; therefore, if an adult is to communicate effectively with them, they need to use a similar kind of language. This perhaps suggests that natural forms of communication between adults and children, commensurate with the child's language at different stages, are beneficial.

## Language acquisition and the development of speaking and listening skills

One of the most important aspects of learning to talk is the ability to hold a conversation that requires the learning of many sophisticated under-standings. In early years settings the ability to take turns with resources without having a tantrum to get your own way, or without thinking about how another person might feel if you take something away from them simply because you want to play with it and, as a child gets older, some-times having to signal that you want to speak by putting your hand up, are examples of important areas that differ significantly from the home language environment. There are many conventions, such as manners, that have to be learned. Children also learn that language differs according to who they are talking to. In this respect, a conversation with an adult will be different to talk with their peers.

Discourse development, which is a particularly important aspect of language, is served by development in all other areas of language develop-ment: syntactic, morphological, lexical and phonological. The main stages of children's syntactic development begin with single words and then move on to two-word phrases. After this, children's syntax develops rapidly and on many fronts. Negative sentences such as 'I am not walking' and the use of complex sentence types will be areas that develop during the nursery stage. The ability to ask questions is another aspect of syntax that develops at this time.

Children's development of morphological understanding can be seen in their capacity to invent words, such as 'carsiz' (cars). The word 'morphological' comes from morpheme. A morpheme is the smallest unit of language that can change meaning. For example if we take the singular 'apple' and turn it into the plural 'apples' then the letter 's' is a morpheme because it changes the meaning from singular to plural. Morphemes that can stand alone, such as 'apple', are called free morphemes, and those which cannot, such as 's' in 'apples' are called bound morphemes.

Lexical development is concerned with the development of vocabulary so is not something that has a particular end point because we continue to add vocabulary throughout our lives. One of the features of children's lexical development is over-extension. An example of over-extension is where children call all meats 'chicken' because they are familiar with that word but not others such as beef and pork. Another feature of lexical development is learning about the way that the meanings of words relate to each other, something called sense relations. Synonyms such as 'happy/joyful' and antonyms such as 'happy/sad' are part of this. This means that children can learn about vocabulary from words that they know without having to directly experience the concept of the word in question.

Phonological development has been much studied, partly because of its link with learning to read (see Section 2 for a detailed explanation of children's developing phonological awareness and learning to read). As far as talk is concerned there are some understandings and skills that have to be acquired before those which are beneficial for literacy. For example, young children learn to control their vocal cords. The sound/airflow which passes from the vocal cords is obstructed in various ways in order to form phonemes (sounds). The place of articulation involves use of the teeth, lips, tongue, mouth and glottis. The manner of articulation involves obstructing the airflow to varying degrees such as completely stopping it or allowing some to pass through the nose.

By examining the stages of language acquisition and beginning to understand the theories of how and why this process takes place, it becomes clear that children's language experiences from birth will be an important factor in their language development. The significance of the way in which adults interact with children at this time should not be underestimated. It has been acknowledged that adults provide a number of important conditions for children as they can:

- provide access to an environment where talk has high status;
- provide access to competent users of language;
- provide opportunities to engage in talk;
- provide responses which acknowledge the child as a competent language user.

(Wray et al. 1989: 39)

In addition, adults model (in an unplanned way) the conventions of language, provide natural feedback on the effectiveness of a child's ability to communicate, scaffold the child's language learning and enable the child to test their current hypotheses about how language works. The ability of adults to take into account the limited abilities of children and adjust their language accordingly so that children can make sense of them is intuitive for most, especially parents and practitioners.

The degree to which a rich language environment assists language development has been well documented. Research studies have established a correlation between home language experiences in the pre-school period and children's literacy progress at school, for example Tizard and Hughes (1984) and Wells (1986). Both document the influence of home language experiences from birth on a child's ability to use language and communicate effectively. Wells' study, for example, found a direct correlation between children's rates of progress in language learning and the amount of conversation experienced with their parents and other members of their family circle. The quality of social experience and interaction will vary greatly between children, and during the early years, practitioners need to be aware that some children will appear to be confident, articulate masters of the English language, whereas others seem less comfortable language users. However, practitioners should beware deficit models and remember that it is too easy to label a child's spoken language as 'poor', or even to say that they have 'no language', without sufficient thought. It is important then that practitioners understand about language diversity and the ways in which judgements are made about speakers in the classroom. From this perspective it is equally important that practitioners recognise their own histories and status as language users, and resist the temptation to impose their own social criteria on the child's ongoing language development. As Bearne points out:

Language diversity is deeply involved with social and cultural judgements about what is valuable or worthy [...] Judgements are often made about intelligence, social status, trustworthiness and potential for future employment on the basis of how people speak – not the content of what they say, but their pronunciation, choice of vocabulary and tone of voice. Such attitudes can have an impact on later learning.

(Bearne 1998: 155)

## Language development, speaking and listening and the EYFS

Siraj-Blatchford and Clarke (2000: 20) argue that 'language involves more than learning a linguistic code with which to label the world or to refer to abstract concepts; language also involves learning how to use the code in socially appropriate and effective ways.' From a very early age, children are learning through language, they are learning to use language, and they are learning about language. In the early years setting, children

- develop their knowledge and understanding about how language works;
- develop a range and variety of vocabulary to use;
- develop awareness of their audience – whom they are speaking to (there is some evidence to suggest that by the age of four, children have learned to adjust their speech according to different audiences);
- think about the appropriate language to use according to the circumstances of the situation;
- learn to speak coherently and with clarity to make themselves understood;
- learn to speak with confidence.

Purposeful language situations must be planned in order for children to practise their language skills and become aware of what is appropriate or suitable for a specific context. Children need to learn to take turns, negotiate, share resources, listen to and appreciate another person's point of view and function in a small group situation. Opportunities for purposeful language situations are many; in role play areas, for example, or round a talk table. Collaborative interaction can be encouraged round the water and sand trays. If there are two chairs by the computer, one child can discuss with another the programme they are using, and children can also learn to wait for their turn (the use of a sand timer to make the waiting time fair can help). The practitioner can skilfully draw children into various activities and discussions in the setting, both indoors and outdoors.

Children need to know that the setting is a place where emotions can be expressed. It is the ability to manage some of these emotions through talk that is the challenge both for the individual child and the practitioner. Young children are naturally physically expressive, for example, when tired, upset or happy, yet they do not always understand straight away the meaning another child is conveying and sometimes need support or reinforcement to encourage more appropriate behaviour. For example, young children experience an intense sense of injustice if they feel they have been wronged. Consider the scenario where one child hits another who immediately responds by hitting back. The practitioner must aim to support the child to use language as a tool for thinking by encouraging the child to ask the following kinds of questions: Why did they hit me? Did I do anything to provoke or upset them? Why am I upset? How should I respond to being hit? What should I do if this happens again? A strong early years setting will provide guidelines for children to follow or appropriate support systems if they find themselves in this kind of situation. In a situation of conflict it can be useful when practitioners point out the expression on a 'wronged' child's face to highlight the consequences of someone else's actions. Conversely, if a child is kind to another child and that child stops crying or starts to smile, then this too can be highlighted.

Non-verbal language such as facial expression, effective eye contact, posture, gesture and interpersonal distance or space is usually interpreted by others as a reliable reflection of how we are feeling (Nowicki and Duke 2000). Mehrabian (1971) devised a series of experiments dealing with the communication of feelings and attitudes, such as like and dislike. The experiments were designed to compare the influence of verbal and non-verbal cues in face-to-face interactions, leading Mehrabian to conclude that there are three elements in any face-to-face communication: visual clues, tone of voice and actual words. Through Mehrabian's experiments it was found that 55 per cent of the emotional meaning of a message is expressed through visual clues, 38 per cent through tone of voice and only 7 per cent from actual words. For communication to be effective and meaningful, these three parts of the message must support each other in meaning; ambiguity occurs when the words spoken are inconsistent with the tone of voice or body language of the speaker.

Similarly, the practitioner needs to be aware of the messages they are sending out to a child via their use of non-verbal language. It is important to remember that whenever we are around others we are communicating non-verbally whether we want to or not, and children need to feel comfortable in the presence of the adults around them. According to Chaplain (2003: 69), 'children are able to interpret the meaningfulness of posture from an early age.' Even locations and positions when talking can be important. For example, it is beneficial when speaking with young children to drop down to their level, sitting, kneeling or dropping down on one's haunches alongside them. This creates a respectful and friendly demeanour and communicates a far more genuine interest in children and what they are doing than bending over them from on high. The way practitioners communicate with children is therefore a very important part of their role. Some suggestions include:

- ensuring that when you talk with children they feel that you respect them, are interested in them and value their ideas;
- giving children your full attention as you talk with them; using direct eye contact to show that you are really listening;
- finding ways of encouraging children to talk in a range of contexts;
- using specific positive praise such as 'I really liked the way that you waited patiently for your turn on the computer';
- smiling!

The specific chapters related to speaking and listening in this book include practical activities and techniques to encourage speaking and listening in the early years as well as suggestions to support home links with parents and carers.


## Pointers for speaking and listening in the early years

In order to develop and consolidate their language skills, young speakers and listeners need:

- to feel safe and secure in their early years environment;
- to build relationships of trust and understanding with their key worker or practitioner;
- to have access to a wide variety of resources and activities to encourage, develop and support speaking and listening skills;

- to have constancy and consistency in terms of opportunities and situations in which to develop their speaking and listening skills (consider a whole-setting policy);

- to participate in an environment rich in speaking and listening opportunities.


## Conclusion

Children's language acquisition is likely to be stronger if they are encouraged to become active participants in conversation, if they are encouraged to be questioning (despite how frustrating this can be for some adults to deal with), to hypothesise, imagine, wonder, project and dream out loud, and to hear stories and to tell stories to others. The social and cultural aspects of language development are equally important at this time, as children learn, through talk, to place themselves within a specific social context, and in this way the development of language and identity are closely linked. The impact of what is happening in any child's home life should never be underestimated, and it is important for the practitioner to take the time to get to know individual circumstances in order to respond supportively. Once children begin to feel emotionally secure in their early years setting, the scene is set for further learning to take place. Here is an overview of practical ways to support speaking and listening in your setting:

- Read story books aloud to children and ask questions to enhance their understanding of the text. Talk with them about what they think is happening in the story. Ask open-ended questions to encourage predictive skills such as 'What do you think is going to happen next?' Include rhymes and poems as part of your reading repertoire.

- Sing action songs and nursery rhymes with the children so that they experience role play and music and develop their awareness of rhyme.

- Use story sacks in your setting. A story sack is a large cloth bag containing a good quality story book with supporting materials, such as puppets and soft toys that act as visual aids to tell the story. It includes a non-fiction book related to an aspect of the story, and there is also a game to stimulate language activities. Finally, there is a cassette tape or CD with the story recorded onto it so children can listen and follow along with the story book.

- Make puppets a part of your setting or classroom. Most young children lose their inhibitions with puppets and talk to them as if they were real. Use them to gain children's attention and as part of your teaching during a whole class input. Put out a puppet theatre in your setting or classroom and observe the children's collaborative play, or put puppets in your book corner and observe the children reading to them!

- Set up areas of the setting or classroom to support and encourage collaborative talk such as role-play areas that reflect children's life experience and interests such as a post office or a café. Use role play constantly.

- Include a talk table in your setting or classroom. Put out the visual aids from the story sack you are using, for example, and encourage the children to retell the story.

- Use show and tell where children talk to the rest of their peers about an object that they have brought in from home.

- Plan specifically for adult–child interaction, for example devising adult-focused activities where children work with the practitioner on a one-to-one basis.

- Have a listening area in your setting or classroom where children can listen to pre-recorded stories or music via headphones.

- Use talk partners to encourage children to verbalise and clarify the thoughts in their head during whole-class discussion and before independent writing.

- Play board games with the children to encourage turn taking.

## 2 Linking sounds and letters and reading: beginner and developing reader behaviours

Hall (1987) defined children's early reading and writing behaviour as emergent literacy. Superseding the view that literacy developed only in response to systematic instruction, emergent literacy explores the reading and writing behaviours of young children that precede and develop into conventional literacy from birth onwards. Hall defined emergent literacy thus:

> It implies that development takes place from within the child [...] 'emergence' is a gradual process. For something to emerge there has to be something there in the first place. Where emergent literacy is concerned this means the fundamental abilities children

have, and use, to make sense of the world [...] things usually only emerge if the conditions are right. Where emergent literacy is concerned that means in contexts which support, facilitate enquiry, respect performance and provide opportunities for engagement in real literacy acts.

(Hall 1987: 9)

Emergent literacy encompasses two important concepts:

1 Young children as being literate rather than becoming literate before they enter formal schooling.
2 Young children as active participants in the construction of their own knowledge about literacy.

The term further encompasses the view that the literacy practices and products of early childhood must be acknowledged as valid in their own right rather than perceived as inadequate manifestations of adult, or conventional, literacy (Gillen and Hall 2003). Teale and Sulzby (1986) came to several research-based conclusions about early literacy development which they suggest underpin emergent literacy:

1 Literacy development begins before formal literacy instruction starts.
2 Literacy development is to do with learning about the functions and forms of literacy and children use a wide variety of reading and writing behaviours in the informal contexts of family and community.
3 The cognitive activities that occur before schooling are an essential part of literacy learning.
4 Children learn literacy through engaging with adults in a literate world.
5 Although there are recognisable stages through which children's literacy learning passes, individuals go through these stages in a number of ways and at different ages.

## Emergent literacy and early reading

Emergent literacy suggests that literacy development will occur wherever literacy practices are taking place: thus, children begin to learn about reading and writing initially in their homes and communities through interacting with others in reading and writing situations. Participation in reading practices represents an important phase of literacy learning for children. It is through such participation that they come to understand important concepts about how reading 'works' (Neuman and Roskos 1997). Children come to understand that print is meaningful, for example:

- that written text conveys a message;
- that writing in books and in the environment is made up of separate words that correspond to spoken words;
- that those words remain the same every time they are read;
- that words are made up of individual letters;
- in English, that texts are read from left to right.

Studies from the English-speaking world have pointed to the advantages for young children of family involvement in their literacy development (e.g. Hannon et al. 1991). Neuman and Dickinson (2001) argued that the pre-school years play a critical role in children's general long-term literacy success, and several research studies have consistently established a correlation between home literacy experiences in the pre-school period and children's literacy progress (Teale and Sulzby 1986; Purcell-Gates 1986; Neuman and Roskos 1997; Kirkpatrick 2001; Dunsmuir and Blatchford 2004). Teale and Sulzby (1986) argued that the home environment can be the source of three broad categories of literacy experiences:

1 those in which children interact with adults in reading and writing situations;

2 those in which children explore print on their own;

3 those in which children observe adults modelling literate behaviours.

The social-class dimension of family literacy practices has long been recognised as a major influence on young children's literacy development (Heath 1983; Brooker 2002), and it is known that children from lower-income families consistently perform lower on literacy measures than their middle-class counterparts (see, for example, Gregory 2001). As Gregory has argued, however, this does not mean that parents from certain social classes do not provide their children with experience of a rich variety of home and community activities and cannot support their children. Nutbrown and Hannon (2003), for example, conducted a study of the family literacy practices of seventy-one five-year-old children drawn from areas of low social and economic deprivation and of low literacy achievement in an English city. These children were reading with their parents, including one-quarter (25 per cent) of the sample who were reading on a regular basis with their fathers.

Current research suggests that it is the quality and frequency of the literacy-related interactions and activities that children experience at home that makes a difference to children's short- and long-term outcomes. Purcell-Gates (1986) documented the ways in which print was used in the homes of twenty low-income families in the USA. Between them, the families had a total of twenty-four children aged between four and six. Purcell-Gates explored relationships between how print was used by the families and the children's emergent literacy knowledge. The families were observed intensively over a one-week period. The study revealed a great variability in types and frequency of literacy events across the twenty homes, and Purcell-Gates was able to establish three patterns of relationships between home literacy practices and emergent literacy knowledge:

1   Children's understanding of the intentionality of print was related to both the frequency of literacy events in the home and to their personal involvement and focus on the literacy events.

2   Children knew more about the alphabetic principle and the specific forms of written language in homes where literate members read and wrote for their own entertainment and leisure.

3   Parents' intentional involvement in their children's literacy learning was higher when their children began formal literacy instruction in school.

Purcell-Gates reached a general conclusion that children of pre-school age who have begun to construct knowledge about the forms and concepts of written English and its alphabetic nature will begin formal literacy instruction in school with schemata for literacy which puts them at an advantage over their peers who have yet to begin this learning (1986: 426).

Wells (1986) discovered a very strong relationship between knowledge of literacy at age five and all later assessments of school achievement leading him to conclude that differences between children's abilities were strongly associated with family background. Wells looked at how the children in the study might have discovered something of the significance of written language before they came to school. He established that the parents' own interest in literacy was important – for example, the number of books that they owned and how much reading and writing happened at home (both with their children and for themselves). He found evidence showing that the children in the study were learning and experimenting using the example of models provided by adult behaviour. Wells also highlighted the importance of the child's own interest in literacy as being significant in relation to progress made at school, suggesting that a less rich literacy environment at home does not always predict a negative impact for a child's future literacy development. He referred to the children in the study as 'meaning makers', a term used to describe the active role that they took not only in relation to their attempts to make sense of their world, but also with regard to their own learning.

Collins and Svensson (2008) explored the reading behaviours of ten 'competent' nursery and reception children from different socio-economic backgrounds, identified as reading in advance of their peers. Findings showed that there was a commonality of approach within the families of the children, even though they came from different socio-economic backgrounds (Collins and Svensson 2008: 90). The children were used to sharing and talking about books, for example, and reading was part of everyday practice at home. In addition, the children were aware of the significance of print around them (environmental print). They were used to playing word games and had been taught familiar songs and rhymes; all of which, the authors argued, contributed to their more advanced reading skills.

## The importance of story and reading with children

Wells' (1986) longitudinal study investigated the influence of the home during the pre-school years on children's long-term literacy development from the start of speech to the end of their primary education. Although the main focus of the study was an investigation of language development in the years prior to school entry, Wells also looked at what was required for children to be able to extend their command of language in relation to reading. One of his main conclusions was the importance of being read to. He argued that listening to stories read aloud gives children experience of the organisation and structures of written language and that through listening to stories children are able to develop their mental model of the world and a vocabulary necessary to talk about it. Listening to stories also leads to the opportunity for collaborative talk between children and parents; children can relate to the stories and understand the significance of the events recounted within them in the light of their life experience and vice versa, a view supported by Purcell-Gates (1986). She argued that children who were consistently read to possessed a greater understanding of the difference between the conventions of written and spoken language.

## The development of phonological awareness: linking sounds and letters

(For some key technical vocabulary please see Appendix.)

Shankweiler and Fowler (2004: 483) argued that children's early awareness of the phonemic principle of alphabetic writing 'plays a central role in becoming a skilled reader of English and other alphabetic systems'; however, there are stages of phonological awareness that children must go through in relation to language development before they are ready to receive specific phonics instruction. The section in the practice guidance for the EYFS (DfES 2007b) that relates specifically to developing phonological awareness is entitled 'Linking Sounds and Letters'. The guidance supports an initial multi-sensory approach that relates in particular to Phase 1 of Letters and Sounds, the government-produced systematic synthetic phonics programme (DfES 2007), where children learn variously from simultaneous visual, auditory and kinaesthetic activities designed to secure their essential phonic knowledge and skills. These activities begin from birth by encouraging babies to use their voices to make sounds and babbling noises. Babies are also encouraged to listen to the intonations and sounds of the voices of their carers, thus supporting their potential from the outset to discriminate with regard to the sounds, rhythms and patterns (particularly) of the English language. Children learn to use words to speak and understand from a very early age that they have the ability to communicate meaningfully using approximations, single and, eventually, combinations of words (see Section 1 for an overview of this theory). Those words can then further be broken down into various constituents or phonological units in different ways. Shankweiler and Fowler (2004) argued that such sensitivity to larger phonological units including words, rhymes and syllables, occurs earlier and probably more naturally than awareness of individual phonemes.

Research evidence suggests that once children understand how to discriminate whole words they will then have the potential to be able to learn to break them down into smaller units, for example into syllables (see Goswami and Bryant 1990). Simple games such as clapping the number of syllables in a child's name (e.g, three claps for Jon-a-than) or similarly shaking a musical instrument once for every syllable are common practice in early years settings. The teaching and use of rhythm and rhyme pervade the practice guidance for children aged sixteen months and above in the 'Linking Sounds and Letters' section. The rationale for such an emphasis is that identification of groups of final sounds is important in relation to developing children's phonological awareness. Specific phonics instruction where children learn to hear and say individual sounds in words, link sounds to letters and begin to apply and use their phonic knowledge in practical ways begins between the ages of forty and sixty months according to the practice guidance. What this means in relation to reading is that children need to learn that phonemes should be blended, in order, from left to right, from the beginning of a word through to the end; and in relation to writing, that words can be segmented into their constituent phonemes for spelling. Segmenting phonemes is the reverse of blending phonemes to read words. Systematic phonics teaching is necessary for children because their explicit awareness of the phonemic structure of words does not come about simply as they gain maturity and experience with the spoken language; 'most children need to have phoneme structure pointed out to them in order to make sense of the mappings between phoneme segments and corresponding letters' (Shankweiler and Fowler 2004: 489).

## Early reading and the EYFS

Children should be encouraged to see books as part of everyday life from birth, and books should be incorporated within their early years settings as an integral part of everyday practice. There are now some very sophisticated and appropriate books available for babies and toddlers (see in particular the main story books referred to and the reading lists for the age range 'From birth–20 months' in each chapter). From about thirty months onwards, most children are at the stage of role-play reading. In this phase, they are readers in so far as they show an interest in books and the print they see around them. They imitate the things they see adult readers doing such as holding a book carefully, turning the pages and talking out loud as they do so. They often retell stories they have heard as they pretend to read. They may read to their cuddly toys, dolls, friends or younger siblings. In the early years setting, children should:

- be exposed to sounds, rhymes, poems, stories and songs from birth;
- be encouraged to respond to the stories, songs and rhymes that they hear and develop a repertoire of favourites;
- select favourite books to be read and reread to them;
- begin to retell favourite stories whilst still unable to read conventional text;
- develop an increasingly sophisticated knowledge and understanding of the way texts work, including responding to the sub-texts of illustrations;
- come to understand that writing and drawing are different, for example, pointing to the text and asking for 'the black bits' to be read;
- develop their curiosity about print, for example, asking 'What does this say?';
- begin to recognise and name some letters;
- react to environmental print, for example, a supermarket bag or shop sign;
- talk about their own experience and relate it to the story being read, for example, 'That looks like my dog';
- learn to approach reading with confidence;
- develop their ability to read conventionally at their own pace.

In order for children to progress, reading activities need to be embedded in children's preferred experiences and interests if they are to be valuable (Miller and Smith 2004).

## Pointers for linking sounds and letters and reading in the early years

In order to develop and consolidate their reading skills, beginner readers need:

- to be treated as readers from the outset;
- to see reading as part of everyday life;
- to have access to a wide variety of resources and activities to encourage, develop and support their interest in print and their reading skills;
- to be encouraged to join in with texts and read too;
- to see that reading is enjoyable and purposeful (children who are more interested in reading will make use of the opportunities and experiences that are offered to them);

- to be offered play-based reading opportunities which are grounded in meaningful contexts;

- to have constancy and consistency in terms of opportunities and situations in which to develop their reading skills;

- to participate in an environment rich in reading opportunities.

The specific chapters related to linking sounds and letters and reading in this book include practical activities and techniques to encourage children's reading development in the early years as well as suggestions to support home links with parents and carers.

## Conclusion

Learning to read conventionally is a process that develops over a period of time. It begins as soon as a child starts to show an interest in books, for example, choosing a particular story for you to read to them. It is important to develop children's confidence in themselves as readers, and there are several ways that they can be supported and encouraged to develop their early reading skills. If children are supported appropriately in their early efforts to read, eventually they will become proficient readers. It is therefore important to develop children's confidence as readers. Reading contexts must be planned in order for children to practise their reading skills. Remember that the main goal is to instil a love of books and reading. Here is an overview of practical ways to support beginning reading skills in your setting:

- Read to children as often as you can. Make looking at books part of the daily routine.

- Draw attention to the illustrations when reading to children.

- Encourage children to choose the books you read together and to tell the story from the illustrations in the book.

- Talk about the books you read and the people, things and animals in them. Make observations, for example, 'This looks like it's going to be a funny story!'

- Resource the setting with books that will describe familiar experiences, concepts and objects as well as fairy tales and fantasy stories.

- Make use of audio tapes and CDs of favourite stories and songs within the setting in a listening area. Use headphones if necessary so the children can listen to tapes and CDs without disturbing others around them. Put copies of the text out in the listening area so that children can begin to understand the concept of turning the page to follow the story.
- Help children to recognise their own name.
- Teach children nursery rhymes and songs.
- Select books that use repetition to capture the rhythm of language, for example, 'The Three Billy Goats Gruff'.
- Hold books so that children can see the pictures and writing. Point to the words as you read.
- Invite children to hold the book and turn the pages.
- Encourage children to join in and read too.
- Plan and model reading for everyday situations: for example, 'Today we are going to make a cake. Let's read the recipe together'.
- Accept and praise children's attempts to read. Treat them as if they are already readers. If they say, 'I'm reading', say 'What are you reading?' or 'Can you read your story to me?'

## 3 Writing and handwriting: beginner and developing writer behaviours

### Emergent literacy and early writing

Rather than portraying them as being unable to write, emergent literacy sees young children instead as having had relatively little experience of writing (Whitehead 2002). Emergent literacy establishes the fact that children will already be experimenting with mark-making and writing from a very early age, before they begin to use the alphabetic principle of letter–sound relationships and despite the fact that the writing produced might not be conventional from the perspective of an adult. Studies spanning a twenty-year period can be found to support this line of thinking. Harste et al. (1984) discovered that children as young as three were already making planned organisational decisions about their writing and that they wrote with an expectation that the marks they made would make sense, a characteristic of the writing process termed 'intentionality'. Many three-year-olds, for example, have developed a mark which to them represents their name. Goodman (1986) argued that children from the age of two engage in writing tasks for a wide variety of reasons and that most have begun to use symbols to represent real things. Lancaster (2003) found that before the age of two children are already able to distinguish between writing, drawing and number. This is based on the child's experience and perceptions of how each of these three domains individually represents meaning. Universal patterns of behaviour reflecting a common set of cognitive processing decisions on the part of children have been identified, such as children making marks that reflect the written language of their culture when asked to write. Such research is important because it suggests that the marks children make on paper are deliberate and purposeful instead of being unorganised and random as they might appear to an inexperienced onlooker.

Many different terms have been used to describe children's early writing behaviour. Clay (1975) referred to children's early attempts to write as beginning writing behaviour, and Martello (2001, 2004) used the term 'precompetence', i.e. children utilising their existing knowledge about writing in order to learn how to write conventionally through choosing what they want to represent and then finding the best possible means in the light of their current literacy knowledge and understanding to represent their intended meaning. Pahl (1999) too has argued that children interpret things according to the information and resources to which they have access at the time and according to what is currently salient in their thinking in this respect; it is inexperience that distinguishes children's ability to make meaning from that of adults more than the strategies they use when they approach a written task. Kress has argued that the signs which children make are, despite their differences from adult forms, fully meaningful in every sense (1996: 17). Kress' argument is somewhat polemical as the signs which children make are not 'fully' meaningful in every sense – otherwise adults would be able to read and interpret them in the conventional way. Whilst his view is important because it underlines the fact that we should view children's early writing as valid, it would be more accurate to say that children's early attempts at writing are meaningful, they are just not conventional.

The writing sample below by Amanda, aged three years and six months, demonstrates this argument well. Clearly she already knows a lot about the conventions of letter-writing. Amanda had written a letter to her daddy at nursery one day and wanted to post it to him. This is how she stamped and addressed the envelope, before folding up her letter and placing it inside the envelope ready to post. She used what she knew and understood about writing (the first two letters of her name were the only letters she could reproduce conventionally at the time) to approach the task. Whilst her address may not be conventionally written, it is certainly meaningfully written.

Clay warned of the consequences of dismissing a child's efforts to put marks on paper, arguing that through close scrutiny of what they had done, one would find a 'rich commentary on their earliest learning about print encapsulated in their accumulated attempts to write' (1975: 15). Clay described the development of writing as a phenomenon that occurs along a continuum, the starting point of which begins with children making 'gross approximations' on paper once they understand that spoken messages can be written down (1975: 15). Gross approximations gradually become more and more refined as children's knowledge about writing develops with more advanced concepts emerging out of earlier understandings (Clay 1975, 1993). This is a view supported by Dyson (2001) who argued that children's writing follows a developmental pathway from less sophisticated to more sophisticated writing, or encoding.

Emergent literacy further promotes the notion of children as active enquirers into the nature and purposes of literacy. Children are strategic literacy learners, able to develop their own theories about how the print world works. Tizard and Hughes (1984), for example, reported on a persistent and logical approach by the children in their study as they tried to make sense of their world. Wray argued, 'Emergent literacy research presents us with a picture of young children actively engaged in constructing their own knowledge about writing, not simply physically, but also cognitively. Learning to write is a thinking process and, therefore, an awareness of what one is doing [...] is an essential component of the process' (1994: 56).

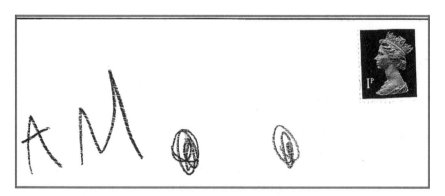

Amanda's stamped and addressed envelope

The portrayal of children as thinking, strategic learners is further supported by psychological studies such as that of McMullen and Darling (2003) who found that typically by the age of three young children begin to think about the problems they need to solve before actually attempting them. The children then utilise what they know in terms of current knowledge and understanding in order to make sense of and apply a strategy to a given situation. McMullen and Darling described this as a definite stage in children's development, where they move on from the more random process of trial and error typically characteristic of children of a younger age when faced with a problem to solve.

To illustrate the concept of children as thinking, strategic learners, a good starting point is to look at a child's knowledge of their name and the significant role it plays in their early writing development prior to their aware-ness of letter–sound development. Personal names provide a way for chil-dren to make sense of the print world as they first recognise their own name; names also become a natural focus for them as they begin to explore written language and a child's own name is often the first word they attempt to write (Clay 1975; Ferreiro and Teberosky 1982; Bloodgood 1999; Yang and Noel 2006). Bloodgood (1999) argued that the name has the potential to enable children to connect literacy strands in a meaningful way. Consequently, it often serves as a tool with which to construct further literacies with the letters in it becoming a common starting point for many types of message (take another look at Amanda's stamped and addressed envelope). It has been argued that when faced with a writing task, children typically solve the problem by apply-ing and using what they know in order to make meaning of the situation. Taking the above example, if all or some of the letters in their name are the only letters they know how to reproduce, children will often re-orchestrate that same set of letters intentionally to produce an infinite number of words. Significantly, whilst each message might look similar, children consider them to be different (Ferreiro and Teberosky 1982).

## Socio-cultural theory and early writing

Current conceptualisations of socio-cultural theory draw heavily on the work of Vygotsky (1986). A key feature of socio-cultural theory is that higher-order functions develop out of social interaction with a more knowledgeable person, either a significant adult (such as a parent or carer) or a peer. Vygotsky (1978) argued that it is when such social interaction with a more competent member of society occurs that cultural knowledge is transmitted to an individual who in turn is able to internalise and incorporate new ideas and concepts into their existing repertoire. A child's development cannot therefore be fully understood by a study of the individual alone because the role of significant adults is a highly influential and important factor. A second key feature of socio-cultural theory is the significance of a social context for development. Development, in terms of young children's strategies for and attitudes to learning, depends on a combination of interaction with (more experienced) people and the tools that a particular culture provides to help children form their view of the world. A third key feature of socio-cultural theory is that knowledge is constructed as a result of the child's active engagement with the environment. Vygotsky (1978) maintained that it is through such active engagement that children's thinking develops, as a result of their ability to assimilate and internalise the processes and practices provided by their socio-cultural context.

Research built on socio-cultural theory shows that children's earliest discoveries about written language are learned through active engagement with both their social and cultural worlds (e.g. Rowe 1994; Gee 2001; Compton-Lilly 2006). By living and participating in an environment in which others use print for various purposes, children infer the semiotic and functional nature of written language (Purcell-Gates 1986: 426). Young children make discoveries about written language in three ways:

1 through interaction with adults in writing situations (Teale and Sulzby 1986);

2 through exploring print on their own (Gregory 2002);

3 through observing adults modelling literate behaviours (Neuman and Roskos 1997).

Neuman and Roskos (1997) argued that participation in writing practices represents an important phase of literacy learning because children come to understand that print is meaningful, and participation enables them to practise what written language is for and how it works. Such shared experiences might include writing a shopping list with a parent before going to the supermarket or writing and posting a birthday card to a relative. Embedding writing experiences in meaningful activity models several distinctive features about it for young children such as the following:

● written text conveys a message;

● writing is made up of separate words that correspond to spoken words;

- words are made up of individual letters;
- in English, texts read from left to right.

Several research studies have suggested that as a result of such individual and shared exploration, children are able to test their hypotheses about the forms and functions of written language in situational contexts from a very early age (Ferreiro and Teberosky 1982; Barrat-Pugh 2002; Rowe 2003). Numerous studies from the English-speaking world have pointed to the advantages for young children of family involvement in their literacy development. Neuman and Dickinson (2001) argued that the pre-school years play a critical role in children's general long-term literacy success, and several research studies have established a correlation between home literacy experiences in the pre-school period and children's literacy progress, including written language development (e.g. Teale and Sulzby 1986; Purcell-Gates 1986; Dunsmuir and Blatchford 2004).

Socio-cultural theories of literacy development also help to explain why children arrive at early childhood settings with different understandings of what writing is (Barrat-Pugh 2002). Whilst there is a regularity that characterises literacy development as shown by those who have defined various stages that children pass through on the road to conventional writing behaviour (e.g. Clay 1975), it is clear that children reach developmental landmarks through a variety of different routes (Pellegrini 2001). Each child's pathway into literacy is a distinctive journey shaped by personal, social and cultural factors (Martello 2002, Whitehead 2002). Socio-cultural theorists see literacy as beginning from birth and argue that what children see as most relevant will differ according to the circumstances of their upbringing; 'learning, especially learning an expressive system like written language, is not divorced from one's identity and history but, of necessity, embedded within it' (Dyson 2001: 139). Children's writing ability is therefore reflective of their socio-cultural past experiences. For writing to become part of a child's communicative repertoire, children need to be in an environment that allows them opportunities to write (Dyson 2001).

## Early writing and the EYFS

In the early years setting, children will:

- begin to mark make from a very early age;
- develop their ability to mark make over a gradual period of time;

- develop their knowledge and understanding about how they can communicate meaningfully through print;
- develop their own personal repertoire of symbolic marks, letters and words to use which will change and become more and more refined over time as their knowledge and understanding of the conventions of writing broadens and as their fine motor and hand–eye coordination skills become more proficient;
- develop awareness of their audience – whom they are writing to, or for;
- think about appropriate marks to make, letters or words to write according to the specific context;
- learn to approach writing with confidence;
- develop their ability to write conventionally at their own pace.

In order for children to progress, writing activities need to be embedded in children's preferred experiences and interests if they are to be valuable (Miller and Smith 2004). Neuman and Roskos (1997) argued that children's earliest discoveries about written language are closely tied to their daily activities as they interact with others in writing and reading situations. They investigated young children's literacy activity within play settings specifically designed to reflect authentic literacy contexts for them. The study acknowledged the role peers can play in a child's literacy development. From observations and taped conversations evidence was found to suggest that more expert play partners, through their more capable demonstrations of 'pretend' play such as how to post letters in a post office, appeared to teach their less-skilled peers, increasing their knowledge of the environment. Hall and Robinson (2003) endorsed the view that literacy activities should be play-based and grounded in meaningful contexts (children's real-world experiences) in order for them to be able to respond to them in a meaningful way and progress.

Below is a writing sample showing how Simon, aged three years and four months, incorporated writing as part of his play one day at his nursery. This is Simon's fire-check register. He had been copying the nursery nurse in his nursery class and taking a class register alongside her on a daily basis for a while using a piece of A4 paper attached to a clipboard and a pen. On this particular day, he told me that there were nineteen children in the nursery. He then decided to dress up as a fireman and did a fire-safety check against the register he had already done. He stood by the name-card board, looked at each name in turn, looked round at his peers in the classroom and then ticked each one off against his register. Observing him, he could not

Simon's fire check register

read the names on the cards apart from his own; however, the principle of one name card for each child present was evident. As you can see from his register, Simon was not forming any recognisable letters; however, he would say each of his peers' names in turn and check them off on his clipboard, using his mark-making skills as a way of recording and communicating meaningfully through print.

Meek sums up the argument in the following quote: 'when writing and reading are correlated with children's intentions manifested in play, young learners will extend their play strategies to encompass the task of learning to make language mean, in both its spoken and written forms' (1991: 98).

## Pointers for writing and handwriting in the early years

Bromley (2006: 15) argued, 'all children, however young, must be given the chance to be seen as writers from the very beginning'. For writing to become part of a child's communicative repertoire they need to be in an environment that allows them opportunities to write (Dyson 2001). Writing behaviour emerges when children have access to writing materials, see models of writing and observe people writing. One of the challenges for early years practitioners is therefore to arrange the most appropriate physical environment to support and include writing experience so as to optimise children's development, for example maximising opportunities to incorporate writing into play. In order to develop and consolidate their writing skills, beginner writers need:

- to be treated as writers from the outset;
- to see writing as part of everyday life;
- to have access to a wide variety of resources and activities to encourage, develop and support their writing skills;
- to be able to choose where they write;
- it would be unwise to restrict writing merely to the writing area, although this is a very important space in the setting. Plan for and include opportunities for writing throughout the setting. Children may be more likely to initiate the need to write for themselves if there are a variety of contexts in which they can use writing for their own purposes;
- to see that writing is enjoyable and purposeful (children who are more interested in writing will make use of the opportunities and experiences that are offered to them);
- to be offered play-based writing opportunities that are grounded in meaningful contexts;
- to have constancy and consistency in terms of opportunities and situations in which to develop their writing skills;
- to participate in an environment rich in writing opportunities.

## Left-handed children

Many children do not establish a preference for using one hand to write with until fairly late in their development. If children seem to prefer using their left hand and are beginning to be interested in writing, here are a few suggested ways to support them.

- Encourage them to sit to the left of right-handed peers so that their arms do not clash.
- Encourage them to position the paper slightly to the left of the centre of their body, tilted clockwise.
- Some left-handed children may need a higher seat to view their work clearly and to ensure a more comfortable writing position, so do experiment with seat height.

Parents should be involved and supported with understanding the writing process. For example, they need to know and understand that in the early stages children's writing will only approximate to conventional writing. The specific chapters related to writing and handwriting in this book include practical activities and techniques to encourage children's writing development in the early years as well as suggestions to support home links with parents and carers.

## Conclusion

Learning to write conventionally develops over a long period of time. It is important to remember that every child progresses at his or her own pace, and what one child is capable of at a certain age may not necessarily be so for another the same age. If children are appropriately supported in their early efforts to write, eventually they will become proficient writers. It is therefore important to develop children's confidence as writers and mark-makers. Writing contexts must be planned in order for children to practise their writing skills and become aware of what is appropriate for a specific context. It should be important not only to listen to children but also to support all efforts to write, if indeed they perceive themselves to be writing. Marks must be valued and interpreted in the light of the context of the writing and the information they give. Here is an overview of practical ways to support beginning writing skills in your setting:

- Find time to show children that you value reading and writing for yourself, and share reading and writing with them. Reading teaches many things about writing and experimenting with writing helps children develop their understanding about reading.

- Read and sing nursery rhymes and books that feature rhyme and repetition.

- Talk about print in the environment, for example, stop signs and advertisements.

- Children learn by listening, watching and copying. Write messages and lists in front of them and talk about what you are doing.

- Provide a writing area in your early years setting. Include a range of writing materials such as plain, coloured or lined paper, crayons, envelopes, diaries and notebooks.

- Make books together. Put book-making resources in your writing area.

- Encourage children to write their own name on their work. If this is a mark that they use consistently, value their efforts and praise them for what they have done (from the age of three years, Amanda used first 'A' and then 'AM' on all her work). Make sure children can access their name cards independently to support their early efforts.

- Use magnetic or plastic letters creatively in the setting: in the sand, in the water, with play dough, etc.

- Allow children to use a computer keyboard. They may discover some letters from their own name.

- When children draw or paint pictures, ask them what it is about, and write down what they say on their drawing.

- Make it clear that you value children's writing, whatever stage of development they are at.

# Language for communication

## From birth–20 months

### *Development matters*

- Communicate in a variety of ways including crying, gurgling, babbling and squealing.

- Make sounds with their voices in social interaction.

- Take pleasure in making and listening to a wide variety of sounds.

- Create personal words as they begin to develop language.

### *Key words*
communicate, interaction, sounds, pleasure

## Main story: *Baby Touch Noisy Book*
**(Justine Smith and Fiona Land (2007), Ladybird, London)**

A bright, colourful first play board book with interactive features. Each page is entitled, 'Baby, touch', 'Baby, say' or 'Baby, listen.' Baby is invited to touch and investigate different textures such as the fur on 'the furry caterpillar'. A button can be pressed throughout on each 'Baby, listen' page to hear a musical version of 'I'm a Little Teapot.' The text invites discussion with the top end of the age range that will link in with some of the children's first experiences of living and learning.

## Activities

- Have a good look through the book before you use it with babies and toddlers to find out what may be appropriate to concentrate on with them. You are aiming to encourage verbal responses from each page – either sounds or words depending on the age of the child.

- Press the 'noisy' button and listen to the rhyme. Press the button again and sing the rhyme. You can do this as many times as the baby or young child seems interested! Children nearer the top of the age range can sing the rhyme with you, or independently. Be prepared to hear the same tune again and again as very young children will be drawn to the novelty feature of the musical button in the book. In fact, through general reading, the book invites six opportunities to use the button and sing along noisily to the tune!

- Open the book and be guided by the text. Use the words on the page as pointers to investigate opportunities for potential responses from the children. For example, the first page suggests they 'touch the furry caterpillar'. Place baby's hand on it and use a stroking motion whilst saying 'ah'. Use words to describe how it feels such as 'soft' and 'silky'. What response do you get? Look for non-verbal clues such as smiles, gurgles and other noises and eye contact with the page. Ask the children at the top end of the age range to describe themselves how the furry caterpillar feels.

- Say the simple rhyme on the first page, 'The peas in the pod go pop, pop, pop', and clap your hands once for every 'pop'. Encourage older children in the age range to join in.

- Sing the octopus's noisy song on the second page (press the button and sing 'I'm a Little Teapot' loudly). Do this for every noisy song on every 'Baby, listen' page as you progress through the book together.

- Use visual aids alongside the text such as a train on a track that you can model moving along as you read the fourth page together. Older children will be able to move the train for themselves. Say 'Clickety clack, clickety clack' as they do so.

- The seventh page is entitled 'Baby, say.' The idea is that the child learns to hear and then to make appropriate sounds associated with each of the four animals: the clippety-clop of the horse's hooves on the ground, the moo of the cow, the baa of the sheep and the woof of the dog. Use a puppet or soft-toy version of each animal to support the activity. This will give further opportunities for the children to touch and investigate textures and talk about how those textures feel.

- Remember to model any suggested actions throughout such as waving to the baby (p. 2), clapping hands (p. 5), waving to the butterfly (p. 8), whispering (p. 9).

## Key questions

- Can you press the button?

- What can you hear?

- Would you like to touch the furry caterpillar/sparkly helicopter, etc.?

- What does it feel like?

- Can you wave to the baby (p. 2)?

- Where are the giraffes (p. 3)?

- What noise does the horse/cow/sheep/dog make?

- Can you sing the song with me?

## *Look, listen and note*

Observe and note the children's responses when you share stories with them. Even at this early age they will be developing favourites that they will wish to return to time and time again.

## Effective practice

- Find creative ways to share stories such as using puppets and other visual aids as well as musical instruments.

- When children do repeat noises such as the animal sounds that you make, say, 'That's right! The cow goes moo!' to reinforce and support their language development and encourage further inter-action. Do the same with real words and approximations of words.

- Share books as part of daily practice and routine. Find somewhere comfortable where both you and the children can relax and enjoy a variety of story books.

## Planning and resourcing

Make a well-resourced book area a priority for your setting. Develop a collection of supporting resources.

## Home links

- Encourage parents and carers to share books at home with their children.

- Encourage them to read with intonation and, for example, to make the animal or other appropriate noises!

- Support sound association by using soft toys and/or puppets when sharing stories.

- Create simple story packs for parents and carers to use at home with their children, for example the book and the main character cuddly toy.

## Additional resources

- *Baby Touch Noisy Book* comes as part of an extended series by Ladybird designed to support first discoveries and experience. The interactive nature of the books also supports the development of gross motor and cognitive skills in babies and encourages interaction between the reader and the baby. Here are a few examples, but if you want to look at more, go to www.whsmith.co.uk.

- Land, Fiona (2007) *Baby Touch Colours,* London: Ladybird.

- Land, Fiona and Smith, Justine (2007) *Baby Touch Playtime,* London: Ladybird.

- Smith, Justine (2007) *Baby Touch Playbook,* London: Ladybird.

# The EYFS principles

The above activities support children's development of a secure relationship with their key carer in the setting. They acknowledge that the foundations for learning begin at birth. They allow for children to be treated as individuals with individual needs that can be accommodated and planned for.

# From 16–36 months

## Development matters

- Use single words and two-word utterances to convey simple and more complex messages.

- Understand simple sentences.

- Learn new words very rapidly and are able to use them in communicating about matters that interest them.

## Key words
simple, communicating, interest

# Main story: *The Pop-Up Dear Zoo*
**(Rod Campbell (2004), Campbell Books, London)**

A lift-the-flap version of the classic story about finding the perfect pet. It takes a little while for the zoo to get it right and there are a few surprise animals along the way! Children can lift the flaps to see what the surprise animals are.

## Activities

- Share the story on a one-to-one basis. Let children pull open the flaps to discover the hidden animals. Read all the clues on the zoo crates. Point to the text as you read.

- Revisit the story. This time ask open-ended questions such as, 'Which animal was in this crate?' Talk about the clues on the crates. Read with clear intonation and use actions to denote big, tall, fierce, grumpy, scary, naughty, jumpy and perfect. If your setting uses sign language as part of everyday communication skills with children, use appropriate signs to support the story as you read together.

- Another way to retell the story is to have a basket full of the animals in the story. You will need an elephant, a giraffe, a lion, a camel, a snake, a monkey, a frog and a puppy. Ask the child to find the correct animal and take it out of the basket as you read the story through. You can then talk about each one at the end of the story and retell it without using the book. Keep sending the 'wrong' animals back into the basket until you have only the puppy left. Let the child play with the puppy and talk about how you would look after a dog at home. Perhaps some of your children do have dogs or other pets at home and so can incorporate personal experience into their learning.

- Put out a toy zoo for the children to play with. Encourage them to name the animals in the zoo. Link back to the story; talk about the 'tall giraffes' and the 'fierce lions', for example.

- Put out a vets' surgery for the children to play with.

- Create a display of zoo animals and a display of pets.

## Key questions

- Which book is this?

- Which animal do you think we will find under the flap?

- What does it say about this animal?

- Can you turn the page for me?

- Can you remember which animal was in this crate?

- Can you find the elephant in the basket?

- Do you have a pet at home?

- What animals do you have in your zoo?

- Is the dog poorly? How are you going to make him better?

## Look, listen and note

Continue to monitor children's responses to the stories you share with them. Discover what it is that interests them about particular stories; do they have a fascination for wild animals, for example? Are there other stories you could share that follow similar themes?

## Effective practice

Find stories that support children's current and developing vocabulary.

## Planning and resourcing

Support children's storytelling using small-world play resources to encourage them to begin to retell familiar stories with you.

## Home links

- Make sure that you consistently share individual children's personal spoken word banks with parents and carers.

- Ask parents and carers what their children's interests at home are to see if these can be followed up in the setting through the stories that you share.

- Make sure EAL children are being encouraged to speak their first language at home.

## Additional resources

Inkpen, Mick (1991) *Kipper's Toybox,* London: Hachette Children's Books. Simply told, well-illustrated story about Kipper the dog who cannot understand why the number of toys in his basket keeps changing. A mystery needs to be solved! For those children who are fans of Kipper, there are now many more titles to choose from, including *Kipper's Story Collection* by Mick Inkpen, which contains four Kipper stories ('Kipper', 'Kipper's Birthday', 'Kipper's Toybox' and 'Kipper's Snowy Day'), again published by Hachette Children's Books. (See Chapter 5 where 'Kipper's Toybox' is used as the Main Story with the age range 'From Birth–20 months').

Hutchins, Pat (1972) *Titch,* London: Random House Children's Books. Titch is the youngest and smallest in his family. Everything that his older brother and sister have is always bigger and better; they have bigger bikes, kites that fly higher, and instruments that make bigger noises. But Titch plants a tiny seed …

Lacome, Julie (1993) *Walking Through the Jungle,* London: Walker Books. Excellent use of rhyme and simple repetitive language structures to depict the journey of a small child making his way through the jungle. He hears different jungle noises along the way, but the page must be turned to reveal the animal responsible for the noise. Also suitable for a movement session.

(♪)  Martin, Bill Jnr. (1995) *Brown Bear, Brown Bear, What Do You See?* London: Puffin Books. Beautifully illustrated, very simple repetitive rhyme about favourite animals and colours.

Remember to use visual aids, where possible, with these early stories. Puppets by Post do some fabulous resources (www.puppetsbypost.com). Go to places like the Early Learning Centre (www.elc.co.uk) and look in early years educational catalogues.

## The EYFS principles

The above activities support children as individuals by following their interests through and incorporating them as part of their language development, play and learning in the early years setting. Looking at each child as an individual is important as children develop at different rates, and learning occurs best through the creation of meaningful contexts.

## From 30–50 months

### Development matters

- Use simple statements and questions often linked to gestures.

- Use intonation, rhyme and phrasing to make their meaning clear to others.

- Join in with repeated refrains and anticipate key events and phrases in rhymes and stories.

- Listen to stories with increasing attention and recall.

- Describe main story settings, events and principal characters.

- Listen to others in one-to-one or small groups when conversation interests them.

- Respond to simple instructions.

- Question why things happen and give explanations.

- Use vocabulary focused on objects and people that are of particular importance to them.

- Begin to experiment with language describing possession.

- Build up vocabulary that reflects the breadth of their experiences.

- Begin to use more complex sentences.

- Use a widening range of words to express or elaborate on ideas.

### Key words

intonation, rhyme, rhymes, stories, listens, describe, respond, question, experiment, complex sentences, express, elaborate

# Main story: *All Join In*
**(Quentin Blake (1992), Red Fox, London)**

The Big Book version is ideal to use with the following activities. This is a lovely collection of rhymes that invite participation on the part of the audience. Have your instruments at the ready!

## Activities

### Musical rhymes

- Explain that you are going to read some rhymes to the children.

- Have a box of simple musical instruments to hand such as cymbals, beaters and shakers. Make sure you have one for each child in your group as well as one for yourself so that you can model how and when to use them.

- Explain that there won't be time to read all the poems today, because there are seven in the book altogether, which is quite a lot – too many to read all at once! – and you will read the first two today.

- Point out and read the Important Message on the contents page to the children – 'YOU CAN JOIN IN TOO.'

- Explain that you are all going to join in too and to help you do that you are going to need some musical instruments. (NB: decide beforehand whether the children are going to choose their instrument or whether you are going to hand them out yourself. Use very clear and specific language with the children; for example, 'Sandra, it's your turn to come and choose an instrument next' or 'Sandra, I'm going to give you a green shaker to play'.)

- Let the children have a go with their instruments before you begin to read.

- Talk about the sounds they make with their instruments.

- Read the first rhyme, 'All Join In.' Explain that the children will keep hearing the words 'all join in.' When they do, that is the time to play their musical instrument.

- Read the rhyme and model using your musical instrument with the children when you read 'all join in.'

- Read again, encouraging the children to join in with the phrase 'all join in.'

- Read 'Sorting Out the Kitchen Pans.' Make lots of noise using the instruments for sorting out the pans! Again, encourage the children to join in with phrases such as 'DING DONG BANG' and 'BING BONG CLANG.'

- Ask them 'How are you going to make your musical instruments go CLANG?'

- Find as many kitchen pots and pans and wooden spoons as you can and place them on the carpet area of your setting for the children to sort. Have the Big Book clearly displayed on the 'Sorting Out the Kitchen Pans' page. Say the rhyme with the children as they sort the pans and make some noise. Alternatively, take the pots and pans outside!

- Put out the same selection of musical instruments that you used for the original session for the children to access independently. Observe how they use the instruments; do they try to say the 'All Join In' rhyme? On their own? In pairs? In small groups? Do they make up rhymes of their own?

- On one or more occasions read 'The Hooter Song', 'Nice Weather for Ducks', and 'Sliding', encouraging the children to join in and make the sound effects using their voices.

- Get to know 'The Hooter Song', 'Nice Weather for Ducks' and 'Sliding' as part of your repertoire of rhymes that you know off by heart. Use them with the children as time-fillers, for example whilst everyone is waiting to get their coats on to go outside together.

- The final rhyme in the book is also called 'All Join In.' This lends itself well to a movement session. The children can mime the actions and join in with the phrase 'We ALL JOIN IN.'

### Key questions

- Do you know or can you remember any other rhymes?

- What sound does your instrument make?

- Can you play your instruments loudly or softly?

- What kind of a sound is that?

- Are you ready to all join in?

## Look, listen and note

- Pay attention to the vocabulary the children use to describe the sounds their instruments make. Record their language.

- Record children's use of familiar rhymes within the setting.

## Effective practice

Keep revisiting familiar rhymes and stories with repeated refrains. Build up a repertoire of rhymes with actions, for example, 'Incy Wincy Spider'.

## Planning and resourcing

Make sure you have a good selection of rhymes and poetry books in addition to story books to send home as part of a home-setting book scheme. Make sure some of these are dual language to support EAL learners in your setting. Two good websites for good quality dual language texts are www.mantrapublishing.com and www.milet.com.

## Home links

- Have a rhyme of the week for parents and carers to focus on with their children at home.

- Encourage parents and carers to make rhyme bags for the setting. These are small bags with simple resources. For 'Twinkle, Twinkle, Little Star', for example, you would need a bag with a selection of shiny stars.

## Additional resources

### Musical instruments

Musical instruments such as jingle bells and maracas can be bought from the Early Learning Centre (www.elc.co.uk). For multicultural instruments such as bamboo rainsticks and cabassas, go to www.kidslikeme.co.uk.

### Story books

Rosen, Michael and Oxenbury, Helen (1989), *We're Going on a Bear Hunt,* London: Walker Books. Classic, familiar tale of the family who go on a bear hunt through sometimes difficult and scary terrain, including tempestuous weather conditions. They find the bear and run away as quickly as they can, back the way they came! But is the bear really to be feared? Be prepared to return to this text time and time again.

♪ Ahlberg, Janet and Ahlberg, Allan (1999) *Each Peach Pear Plum,* London: Penguin. Beautifully illustrated rhyme. A book version of the game 'I spy with my little eye.' Characters from nursery rhymes and traditional tales such as Tom Thumb and Cinderella are to be found on every page.

♪ Martin, Bill Jnr. (1994) *Polar Bear, Polar Bear, What Do You See?,* London: Puffin. An interactive rhyming story about animals and the noises they make, such as the lion roaring and the snake hissing.

♪ Crebbin, June (1995) *The Train Ride,* London: Walker. The fantastic, rhythmic language of this story echoes the speed and rhythm of the train as it pulls out of the station, gets faster and faster, and then slows down again as it reaches its destination. A child looks out of the window with his mother to see many interesting sights along the way.

♪ Kennedy, Jimmy and Theobalds, Prue (1993) *The Teddy Bears' Picnic,* London: Uplands Books. An excellent story book version of the traditional song that children will love to sing along to.

# The EYFS principles

The rich environment set up by the above activities enables children to access learning, particularly supporting those children with a love of music. Musical instruments could additionally be provided from several cultures for the children to play. Modelling how to use the instruments on the part of the practitioner will give the children confidence to have a go themselves.

# From 40–60+ months

## Development matters

- Have confidence to speak to others about their own wants and interests.

- Use talk to gain attention and sometimes use action rather than talk to demonstrate or explain to others.

- Initiate conversation, attend to and take account of what others say.

- Extend vocabulary, especially by grouping and naming.

- Use vocabulary and forms of speech that are increasingly influenced by their experience of books.

- Link statements and stick to a main theme or intention.

- Consistently develop a simple story, explanation or line of questioning.

- Use language for an increasing range of purposes.

- Use simple grammatical structures.

## Early learning goals

- Interact with others, negotiating plans and activities and taking turns in conversation.

- Enjoy listening to and using spoken and written language, and readily turn to it in their play and learning.

- Sustain attentive listening, responding to what they have heard with relevant comments, questions or actions.

- Listen with enjoyment, and respond to stories, songs and other music, rhymes and poems and make up their own stories, songs, rhymes and poems.

- Extend their vocabulary, exploring the meanings and sounds of new words.

- Speak clearly and audibly with confidence and control and show awareness of the listener.

## Key words

interact, enjoy(ment), listen(ing), taking turns, speak, confidence, awareness

# Main story: *Oliver's Fruit Salad*
## (Vivian French (1998), Hodder Children's Books, London)

Fruit at home for Oliver is not quite the same after having spent time with his grandpa who apparently grows everything himself in his garden. A trip to the fruit section at the local supermarket with his mother enthuses him once more before he reveals that he did not eat any of Grandpa's fruit because he does not like it! Oliver's opinion finally changes when his grandparents visit and persuade him to try home-made fruit salad.

## Activities

- There are many ways in to this story. You could read it with the children at snack time for example, before the children share their fruit together. The children could be encouraged to try some new fruits that appear in the book such as the pineapple that Oliver has never seen in his grandpa's garden. Have as many of the fruits described in the story as you can to support your storytelling. Either put them in a shopping trolley if you have one at your setting as part of your role-play equipment, or in a shopping bag (try to use a 'green' bag rather than a plastic bag). Include a bottle of black-currant juice, a tin of pears and a jar of jam as part of your resources.

- Having read the story with the children, have a fruit-tasting session. Encourage the children to try a new fruit. Encourage them to touch the fruit and describe how it feels. What are the fruits like to eat? Do they taste nice? Are they sweet?

- Read the story with the children and make a fruit salad using some of the fruits described in the story.

- Relate to the children's experiences of eating fruit at home.

- Create your own group or class fruit salad story with the children during a shared writing session. Encourage them to write and illustrate their own fruit salad stories independently: 'Tess's Fruit Salad' or 'Jamil's Fruit Salad' for example.

- Investigate where fruit comes from round the world.

- Make a simple block graph depicting the children's favourite fruit.

- Focus on the 'everyday' elements of the story that the children can relate to: family life, seeing grandparents and carers, going shopping with parents and carers, being at home with parents and carers. Discuss with the children what they do at home with their families. What happens when they go shopping? What do they like to buy?

- Set up a role-play fruit shop in your setting. Make labels for the shop with the children and include pads and pens for them to write their own shopping lists on. Include purses, money, shopping baskets, shopping bags, old receipts and a till.

## Key questions

- What do you think this book is about? (Look at the front cover together, read the title as a clue.)

- Which fruits can you see?

- Do you like fruit?

- What is your favourite fruit? Why?

- Where do you think this fruit is grown?

- Do you think Oliver likes fruit? Shall we find out?

- Why do we need to go shopping?

- Who do you go shopping with?

- What do you like to do at home? Why?

- What is going to happen in your story?

## Look, listen and note

- Are children willing to engage in conversation with you?

- Do they have the language skills and the social skills necessary to be able to converse with you or with other members of their group or class, for example in the role play fruit shop?

- Do you need to adapt/simplify your language?

- Can children take turns in conversation with you and their peers?

## Effective practice

- Interact with the children in the role-play fruit shop. Model appropriate behaviour and language with the children. Bring your own shopping list and ask lots of questions about where you can find certain fruits.

- Encourage the children to share their fruit-salad stories with the group or class.

## Planning and resourcing

Involve the children in the setting up of the role-play fruit shop. Create a list together of what they think they would need for it.

## Home links

- Make sure children are not allergic to some of the fruits you might be using as part of the above activities. Send a letter home or check setting records.

- Invite parents and carers to send in a piece of their child's favourite fruit to share.

## Additional resources

An atlas should be part of the standard provision in your setting book corner. There are many atlases suitable for children these days; here are a couple of suggestions.

- Wright, David and Wright, Jill (2007) *Children's Atlas,* Phillip's.

- Brocklehurst, Ruth and Edwards, Linda (2003) *The Usborne Children's Picture Atlas,* London: Usborne Publishing.

Two very good information book titles are:

- Matthews, Sarah and Valat, Pierre-Marie (1998) *Fruit,* London: Moonlight.

- Houbre, Gilbert and Matthews, Sarah (1990) *Vegetables,* London: Moonlight.

Both these books are part of a series by Moonlight Publishing (www. moonlightpublishing.co.uk) in which children can see the whole or part of each fruit or vegetable through the use of transparent overlays which help to illustrate changes and processes. In *Fruit,* for example, the apple is sliced open, and the reader can see the seeds and what happens when they are planted and grow.

### Story books

- Browne, Eileen (1994) *Handa's Surprise,* London: Walker. Well known multicultural tale of Handa who takes seven pieces of delicious fruit to her friend, Akeyo. (See also Chapter 6 where 'Handa's Surprise' is used as the Main Story with the age range 'From 16–36 Months').

- French, Vivien (1995) *Oliver's Vegetables,* London: Hodder Children's Books. A similar idea to *Oliver's Fruit Salad,* but Oliver learns to like vegetables this time. He refuses to eat anything other than chips, but he plays a game with his grandpa: whatever vegetable Oliver finds in grandpa's garden he must eat! This book also introduces the days of the week.

- Carle, Eric (2003) *The Very Hungry Caterpillar Giant Board Book,* London: Penguin. A giant board book version of the familiar story, which follows the caterpillar's week as he eats through a range of healthy fruit and unhealthy food that gives him a stomach ache, as he prepares for his hibernation and transformation into a beautiful butterfly. A caterpillar toy can be pushed through the holes in the book as the children follow the story. (See also Chapter 4 where *The Very Hungry Caterpillar* is used as the Main Story with the age range 'From thirty to sixty months').

## The EYFS principles

The above activities enable each child to respond as an individual, for example with likes and dislikes regarding the taste of certain fruits and acknowledging different cultures.

# 2 | Language for thinking

## From birth–20 months

### *Development matters*

- Are intrigued by novelty and events and actions around them.

- Understand simple meanings conveyed in speech.

- Respond to the different things said to them when in a familiar context with a special person.

### *Key words*
intrigued, understand, meanings, respond

## Main story: *Baby Touch Peekaboo Book*
**(Anon. (2007), Ladybird, London)**

A bright, colourful, tactile first lift-the-flap board book with simple, meaningful text. Each page is entitled either 'Baby, see' or 'Baby, touch.' There are lots of textures to touch and talk about and giant flaps to lift to discover who, or what, is underneath them. The final flap reveals a mirror to reveal who mummy sees!

## Activities

- This is another book with which it is a good idea to familiarise yourself before sharing. By doing so you can use it appropriately depending on the age, interests and abilities of the child you are reading it with. There are several animals interspersed throughout the book for example.

- Touch the front cover of the book together or move baby's hands over the surface to feel the different textures. The elephant's ears make a noise if pressed hard enough. Talk about the noise together.

- When progressing through the book, read the title of each page to reinforce language understanding and the purpose of each page, i.e. seeing (looking), and touching.

- Lift the flaps for children who cannot yet do this for themselves. They are large and sturdy for little hands, however.

- Look for non-verbal clues from the child such as smiles, gurgles and other noises, and eye contact with the page to gauge their interest.

- Model waving to the baby on pages 1 and 3 to support young children's understanding of how words sometimes link with actions.

- For children at the top end of the age range, incorporate visual aids to support the text such as the bouncy bunny (make it hop) and the tractor on page 3, and the zebra and the giraffe on page 5.

- Play a game of 'Peekaboo' together after sharing the book together.

### Key questions

- What can you see?

- Can you see or show me the smiley starfish, baby, tractor, etc.?

- Where is the bouncy bunny, stripy zebra, etc.?

- Can you wave to the baby?

- Can you wave like this?

- What will we find behind the flap?

- Who will be there?

- Who can you see?

- What do the words say? (*After lifting the flaps*) Shall we find out?

- Can you feel the bumpy octopus, fuzzy caterpillar, furry tiger, sparkly helicopter?

- Who can you see in the mirror?

## Look, listen and note

- Note children's personal responses to the text.

- Do they show interest?

- Do they respond to touching the different textures?

- Do young babies attempt to touch the pages, especially once they are able to sit up independently and are beginning to develop hand–eye coordination?

- Do children towards the top end of the age range understand simple instructions such as waving to the baby?

## Effective practice

Although you are encouraging young children to respond to the text, they will not always do so verbally; they will be able to understand much more than they can express in terms of thoughts and ideas. Look carefully for non-verbal responses to check young children's understanding, especially through the questions you ask.

## Planning and resourcing

Make sure young children have access to books and resources appropriate for their age and which support and extend their interests. Children who are fascinated by wild animals will enjoy this book, for example, but also need to be given opportunities for symbolic play with wild animal models, say at the zoo or in the jungle.

## Home links

- Keep up-to-date with children's interests through regular communication with parents and carers.

- Similarly, if children begin to develop particular interests in the setting make parents and carers aware of the personal choices they are making.

## Additional resources

Look out for the full range of the Baby Touch series by Ladybird (see Additional Resources for 'From birth–20 months' in Chapter 1).

# The EYFS principles

The above activities enable children to develop a secure relationship with their key carer in the setting through working on a one-to-one basis and acknowledge that the foundations for learning begin at birth.

# From 16–36 months

## Development matters

- Are able to respond to simple requests and grasp meaning from context.

- Use action, sometimes with limited talk, that is largely concerned with the 'here and now'.

- Use language as a powerful means of widening contacts, sharing feelings, experiences and thoughts.

## Key words

respond, meaning, context

## Main story: *Tiny Rabbit Goes to a Birthday Party*

**(John Wallace (2000), Puffin Books, London)**

Tiny Rabbit is very excited when he receives an invitation to Blue Mouse's party in the post. At the same time, he starts to worry about things like not having any friends there and not knowing how to play the party games. Even worse, what if he is unhappy and wants to go home? This is a delightful, straightforward story set in a meaningful context that very young children will be able to relate to.

## Activities

- Simply read the story with younger children on a one-to-one basis, turning the pages and enjoying the book.

- Look at the endpapers together and talk about Tiny Rabbit playing with the balloons. Can the children relate to this experience?

- Ask simple questions as you read the story and look at the illustrations together, asking questions such as, 'Where is Tiny Rabbit on this page?', and 'What is he doing here?'

- With children at the top end of the age range, read to them in small groups. Find somewhere comfortable where the children will be relaxed, such as the Book Corner.

- Read the blurb on the back of the book as an introduction to the story. What are some of the children's predictions as to the content in relation to the questions contained in the blurb? Read the book. Were they right?

- Once you have finished the story, use a rabbit puppet so that the children can talk to Tiny Rabbit himself about going to the birthday party. Model asking him questions, such as 'How did you feel when the party invitation arrived in the post?' Ask the children what they would like to ask Tiny Rabbit.

- Talk about the children's experiences of going to parties or of their own parties. What food did they eat? What games did they play? Did they enjoy themselves?

- Use soft toys (up to a maximum of four) to create a tea-party role-play area in the setting. This could be out on the carpet for a couple of days, for example. It does not have to necessarily take over your permanent role-play area.

- To encourage independent mark-making, include materials in the writing area for the children to write lists of people they would like to invite to a party and the food they would like to eat.

- Provide a range of dressing-up clothes for the children to try. How do they feel when they dress up? Use language to encourage responses from the children; say, for example, 'Oh! We have a fireman in our group today!', or 'I can't tell who that is dressed up as a doctor – oh, it's ...! I wondered who you really were.'

- Put out a range of 'presents' with wrapping paper, scissors and tape and support the children's problem-solving skills in thinking and talking through about how best to wrap each one.

## Key questions

- What do you think the book is about?

- What is Tiny Rabbit doing here?

- How do you think Tiny Rabbit feels?

- What could Tiny Rabbit do if he gets to the party and doesn't know anyone?

- Have you ever had a party?

- Have you ever been to a party?

- What was it like?

- What did you do?

- What are you going to use to wrap the present?

- How much paper do you need?

- What else could you use? (e.g., putting the gift in a box and wrapping the box).

## Look, listen and note

Observe how children interact with their peers in small groups reading the story together and during role play. Are they following specific lines of thought in relation to the topic of discussion for example?

## Effective practice

Support children's language for thinking through asking open-ended questions relating to their real-life experiences.

## Planning and resourcing

Make purposeful role play related to children's interests and real-life experiences an integral part of the setting.

## Home links

- Encourage parents and carers to use open-ended questioning at home. Run a short workshop if you feel this would be beneficial.

- Develop times for ongoing discussions with parents and carers so that you are aware of significant events happening at home that you can talk with the children about in the setting.

## Additional resources

McBratney, Sam and Jeram, Anita (1994) *Guess How Much I Love You,* London: Walker. How can you describe or measure how much you love someone? Little Nutbrown Hare and Big Nutbrown Hare do their best to do so until it is time for Little Nutbrown Hare to go to bed. This is a story that will generate discussion related to children's personal experiences of feeling loved and feeling love for others.

Chichester Clark, Emma (1998) *I Love You, Blue Kangaroo!* London: Andersen Press. Story about a child called Lily's attachment to her favourite toy, Blue Kangaroo, told from the point of view of Blue Kangaroo himself. Given lots of new cuddly toys as presents for her birthday, it takes Lily a little while to realise just how much he means to her … Children will all have favourite toys to tell you about.

Hughes, Shirley (1993) *Dogger,* London: Random House Children's Books. Dave loses his favourite toy, Dogger, making him feel very sad. Then everything is wonderful again when Dogger turns up on a stall at the garden fête; but someone else buys him before Dave can get the money! Children will be able to identify with Dave's sadness at losing a favourite cuddly toy.

Cooper, Helen (1997) *The Baby Who Wouldn't Go to Bed,* London: Random House Children's Books. Children will identify with the baby who would prefer to stay up all night rather than go to bed when he is told by his mother. A story that will lead nicely into discussions about why we need to go to bed on time and individual bedtime routines.

Cooke, Trish (2008) *So Much,* London: Walker. A delightful look at Afro-Caribbean family home life. Everybody wants to squeeze, kiss and love the baby so much!

# The EYFS principles

The above activities acknowledge the value of a rich, well-planned environment, for example providing opportunities for talk and the development of thinking skills through relevant role-play activities linked to a theme that the children can relate to through real-life experiences.

# From 30–60+ months

## *Development matters*

- Talk activities through, reflecting on and modifying what they are doing.

- Use talk to give new meanings to objects and actions, treating them as symbols for other things.

- Use talk to connect ideas, explain what is happening and anticipate what might happen next.

- Use talk, actions and objects to recall and relive past experiences.

- Begin to use talk instead of action to rehearse, reorder and reflect on past experience, linking significant events from own experience and from stories, paying attention to how events lead into one another.

- Begin to make patterns in their experience through linking cause and effect, sequencing, ordering and grouping.

- Begin to use talk to pretend imaginary situations.

# Main story: *Biscuit Bear*
**(Mini Grey (2004), Red Fox, London)**

One day a little boy called Horace bakes Biscuit Bear. But Biscuit Bear is lonely, so he sneaks into the kitchen at night to make lots of biscuit-bear friends and creates a circus troupe using lots of sweets and icing! Everything is fine until along comes Horace's dog and Biscuit Bear's friends become a pile of crumbs on the floor. Biscuit Bear decides he must find somewhere safe to be ...

## Activities

- Read the story through with the children. Some of the children may have been to a circus or seen performances on the television; draw on their knowledge and understanding, linking it to the story.

- Follow the story up with *Honey Biscuits* by Meredith Hooper. This book operates on several levels: it is a story, a recipe and an information book all in one. It will give the children background information and support existing knowledge and understanding for several of the following activities.

- Make Biscuit Bear's Circus with the children.

  - Create a recipe card with visual pictures clearly depicting each ingredient and everything they will need to bake the biscuits such as bowls and spoons. The method should be illustrated as well. This will support those children who still need support decoding text to be far more independent during the activity.

- Dress the bears 'in icing of many colours, hundreds and thousands, and candied peel and glace cherries and little silver balls'! Use the illustrations in the book to inspire the children.

- Encourage prediction and descriptive vocabulary throughout the making and baking process, for example, 'What do you think will happen when we mix the butter with the sugar?'; 'What does the mixture look like now?'; 'What will happen when we put the biscuits in the oven?'

- If you feel the children need more practice with a rolling pin and cutters, let them experiment with natural-coloured play dough, which looks like raw biscuit dough. Provide a baking tray for them to put their play-dough biscuits on and a play oven to bake them in.

- Alternatively, create a more permanent Biscuit Bear's Circus using salt dough which can be baked and painted.

  - Make a display in the setting, allowing the children to access the figures.

  - Set some parameters regarding a positive approach to the display such as not being too rough with the figures. Talk these through with the children as a group and create written guidelines together. Word these carefully, for example begin with, 'When playing with Biscuit Bear's Circus, it is a good idea to ...' If one or more of the children ignores the guidelines they will be there to refer back to when issues need to be talked through with them.

- Create a role-play Biscuit Bear bakery in the setting. Provide aprons and chefs' hats, wooden spoons and baking bowls. Use natural coloured play dough for the biscuit mix. Include cutters and rolling pins, baking trays and play ovens.

- Children at the top end of the age range can write their own endings to the story describing the safe place Biscuit Bear found to be.

  - Support children to develop their ideas orally before they write them down.

  - Encourage them to share their ideas with a talk partner before relaying them to the larger group or class.

  - Write some of their ideas down. Children could also share their ideas in small groups with you leading and supporting them.

- Playmobil do some wonderful circus small world play sets, including a tight-rope walker. Consider purchasing some items to encourage and support children's imaginative play.

## Key questions

- Who is Biscuit Bear?

- What is he doing? Why?

- How do you make biscuits?

- What ingredients do you need?

- Have you ever made biscuits at home?

- What do we need to do next?

- What do you think will happen now?

- How is your story going to end?

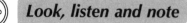

### Look, listen and note

- Observe and record children's use of descriptive language.

- Observe and record children's use of predictive language, how they use talk to connect ideas and explain things.

## Effective practice

Encourage and support children's use of talk to think through and adapt what they are doing through the use of open-ended questioning (What? Why? How?). Try to get behind their lines of thinking based on what they know already.

## Planning and resourcing

Provide plenty of opportunities for shared talk. Use books, small-world play and role-play resources to support children's imagination and willingness to talk with you.

## Home links

- Suggest that parents and carers bake biscuits with their children at home.

- Send home an information leaflet on the use of open-ended questioning.

## Additional resources

Wilkes, Angela (1999) *The Children's Step-by-Step Cookbook,* London: Penguin. This is a good cookbook to give you ideas for cooking in your setting. As well as containing over fifty recipes, the book uses photographs that depict each stage of each recipe as well as ingredients and utensils required. The photographs provide a very helpful visual support for young children who are still learning to read. When using a cookbook in your setting, it is a good idea to use a recipe-book holder. An acrylic one can be found at www.heritage-gifts.co.uk. Make sure you position the recipe-book holder where all the children participating in the cooking activity have a clear view of the recipe.

## Story books

- Macdonald, A. and Rieger, Anja (1999) *The Gingerbread Man,* London: Penguin Books. This version of the classic tale uses rhythmic text to help build reading skills.

- Hooper, Meredith (2005) *Honey Biscuits,* London: Frances Lincoln Publishers Ltd. This book operates on several different levels: it is first a story; second a recipe which can be followed; and third an information book. It provides an insight into where some of the foodstuffs found in every kitchen are provided by the natural world.

- Cooper, Helen (1998) *Pumpkin Soup,* London: Random House Children's Books. The story of three good friends, Cat, Squirrel and Duck, who make the best pumpkin soup together every day. Unfortunately, Duck decides one day that he wants to be Head Cook, leading to all sorts of upset. The story does have a happy ending, reminding the reader what true friendship is all about.

- French, Vivian (1998) *Oliver's Fruit Salad,* London: Hodder Children's Books. Just as an antidote to biscuits! (See also Chapter 1 where *Oliver's Fruit Salad* is used as the Main Story with the age range 'From forty to sixty months').

# The EYFS principles

The above activities provide a language-rich environment in which talk is seen as central to children's learning in terms of both its value and potential. The activities are interesting, exciting and stimulating in order to promote children's talk.

# 3

# Linking sounds and letters

**From birth–20 months**

> ### *Development matters*
>
> - Listen to, distinguish and respond to intonations and the sounds of voices.
>
> - Enjoy babbling and increasingly experiment with using sounds and words to represent objects around them.
>
> ### *Key words*
> listen, distinguish, respond, enjoy, experiment, intonation, sounds

## Main story: *This Little Puffin Finger Plays and Nursery Rhymes*
**(Elizabeth Matterson and Claudia Muñoz (1991), Young Puffin, London, select from the sections 'Baby Games' and 'Nursery Rhymes and Variations')**

This is a fantastic early years collection of appropriate rhymes and songs to use with very young children and includes some of the music for selected rhymes as well as how to do the actions for action rhymes.

## Activities

- Whilst singing and saying action rhymes such as 'This Little Pig Went to Market', and 'Round and Round the Garden', maintain eye contact with babies and smile at them. Create anticipation as the climax of the rhyme approaches. Laugh with the children as they respond in delight.

- As children begin to get slightly older, focus on the words, or approximations of words, that they utter as you enjoy rhymes together.

- Encourage them to join in with some of the actions.

- Always get down to their level; if they are sitting on the floor, sit with them.

- Remember the value of visual aids: develop the use of rhyme bags for example, but remember not to include small parts with children this age that may be unsafe.

- It is important to develop your own repertoire of songs and rhymes to use on a daily basis with children. They can then be used at any moment to calm, soothe or fill in snatches of time.

- Play rhyme CDs, including action rhymes, in the background. Sing along and encourage children to join in with the actions.

### Key questions

- Did you enjoy that song?

- Shall I sing it again?

- Are you going to join in?

- Is that your favourite song?

- Are you talking to me?

- What are you saying to me?

- Shall we play that one again?

## Look, listen and note

Note how children respond to the rhymes you share with them. They will develop favourites very early on. If you keep returning to these, it will help children to feel comfortable and reassured in the setting.

## Effective practice

Remember that strong foundations in a child's home language support the development of English.

## Planning and resourcing

- Expose children to songs and rhymes from other cultures.

- Ensure you support children from all cultures represented in the setting with appropriate resources. Try www.barefootbooks-online.co.uk for a wide selection of songs, rhymes and stories from around the world.

## Home links

- Communicate regularly with parents and carers so that you are aware of the words that children use for things that are special to them as they develop their language skills, such as 'blanken' for 'blanket'.

- Ensure that parents and carers of EAL children are aware of the necessity of speaking their home language with their children.

## Additional resources

(♪)  Roberts, Sheena (2000) *Playsongs: Action Songs and Rhymes for Babies and Toddlers* (with CD), Playsongs. A complete mixed-media product to support baby and toddler action and rhyme development.

(♪)  Gliori, Debi (2005) *Nursery Rhymes* (with CD), London: Dorling Kindersley. Another book that constitutes a complete package with a CD. Children can learn nursery rhymes in a child-friendly way; they are talked through the rhymes by Debi Gliori herself. Includes an introduction to support children following the rhymes in the book. Correct book language is modelled throughout.

(♪)  Scott, Anne and Schwarz-Smith, Lura (2001) *The Laughing Baby: Songs and Rhymes from Around the World,* Berkeley, Calif.: Celestial Arts. Similar to the above, but supporting a more global approach.

(♪)  Anon. (2003) *Animal Boogie,* Bath: Barefoot Books. Book and Music CD featuring animals from the Indian jungle. Play the CD and sing and dance along!

# The EYFS principles

The above activities show how each child can be supported from birth in a positive environment that takes into account their personal preferences. As these are followed through, children are enabled to flourish as individual learners with their own interests, known and understood and planned for on a daily basis by their key workers.

# From 16–36 months

## Development matters

- Listen to and enjoy rhythmic patterns in rhyme and stories.

- Distinguish one sound from another.

- Show interest in play with sounds, songs and rhymes.

- Repeat words or phrases from familiar stories.

## Key words

listen, enjoy, sounds, play, songs, rhymes, familiar stories

## Main story: *Incy Wincy Spider*
**(Jack Tickle and Keith Chapman (2005), Little Tiger Press, London)**

A delightful extended version of the familiar nursery rhyme. For example:

*Incy, Wincy Spider; playing on a farm,*
*Spinning silver silk webs high up in a barn.*
*From an open window a gust of wind blows Whooo!*
*And Incy Wincy Spider with a Whooooosh goes too!*

Incy Wincy Spider is blown from farm animal to animal. An interactive element of the book allows children to trace the sparkling trail of Incy Wincy's web. Where will his journey end?

Here is the traditional version:

*Incy Wincy Spider climbed up the water spout.*
*Down came the rain and washed the spider out.*
*Out came the sunshine,*
*And dried up all the rain.*
*So Incy Wincy Spider climbed up the spout again.*

## Activities

- Make sure you know the traditional version of Incy Wincy Spider. Put some visual aids in a covered story basket: a spider, a water spout (a plastic pipe), a raindrop or picture of the rain and a sun (perhaps from a weather chart in the setting).

- Explain that you are going to sing one of your favourite rhymes with the children.

- Ask them whether they can guess which rhyme it is as you bring out the visual clues one by one.

- Sing the rhyme with the children whilst modelling appropriate actions.

- Give the children musical instruments to use whilst you sing the rhyme together.

- Invite the children to choose and sing their favourite rhymes with you. Continue to play the musical instruments.

- Put spiders and plastic pipes in the water or sand tray for the children to explore.

- Put the visual aids on a talk table so that the children are prompted to recite the rhyme from memory.

- Encourage children to say the rhyme independently; support their efforts by modelling the actions and mouthing the words for the children to follow.

- Now that the children are familiar with the traditional version of the rhyme, introduce the extended version of the rhyme (see Main Story). You can either sing or say it. Use your story basket and fill it with all the animals in the farmyard that Incy Wincy meets along the way: a pig, a goat, a cow, a duck, a horse and a cockerel.

- Read or sing the extended version on a one-to-one basis with children and let them trace their fingers over the (raised) web that Incy creates on each page on his journey to bed. Support children so that they trace the web from left to right, which will reinforce their developing understanding of how in English we read and write from left to right.

- Talk about what will happen to Incy now that he is ready to go to bed. Relate this to what happens at bedtime at home with the children.

- Create a role-play area in which children have the opportunity to put dolls to bed. Include night clothes for them to change the dolls into and toothbrushes, for example. Include a selection of bedtime stories for the children to read to the dolls before they go to sleep.

## Key questions

- Who can guess which rhyme we are going to sing today?

- How do you know?

- What makes you say that?

- What happens to Incy Wincy Spider?

- Can you do the actions with me?

- How could we make some 'rain' music?

- Which instruments could we use?

- Who knows another rhyme?

- Which animal is Incy Wincy Spider going to meet next?

- How do you know?

- Which story are you going to read to your baby?

- What is your story called?

## *Look, listen and note*

Note children's responses to songs and rhymes and focus on these to develop learning. Which are their favourites?

## Effective practice

Encourage children to join in with rhymes, and, when sharing stories, to make different sounds they hear – the noise of the train in *The Train Ride*, for example (see Additional Resources below).

## Planning and resourcing

Include rhymes from different cultures.

## Home links

Ask parents and carers to share their favourite rhymes from their home languages with you.

## Additional resources

You might like to revisit some of the Additional Resources listed in Chapter 1 for the age group 'From 30–60 months' such as *The Train Ride* by June Crebbin and Stephen Lambert and *We're Going on a Bear Hunt* by Michael Rosen and Helen Oxenbury.

(♫) Beaton, Claire (2008) *Playtime Rhymes for Little People,* Bath: Barefoot Books. A delightfully illustrated book of rhymes, accompanied by instructions for acting each one out. The book will help children develop language and counting skills, whilst encouraging coordination and interaction.

(♫) Andreae, Giles and Wojtowycz, David (1998) *Rumble in the Jungle,* London: Orchard Picturebooks. A lovely collection of rhymes about different animals in the jungle, some of which can be used to explore the concept of alliteration or words that begin with similar initial sounds. A Big Book version is now available.

Andreae, Giles and Wojtowycz, David (1999) *The Commotion in the Ocean,* London: Orchard Picturebooks. As above, but with a sea theme. A pop-up version is now available.

Nursery Rhyme Time V2 is an interactive piece of software by Sherston Publishing Group featuring eleven familiar nursery rhymes which can be used with an interactive whiteboard as well as a PC (www.sherston.com).

## The EYFS principles

The above activities continue to support children as individuals in a positive, language-rich environment which takes into account their personal preferences.

## From 30–60+ months

### Development matters

- Enjoy rhyming and rhythmic activities.
- Show awareness of rhyme and alliteration.
- Recognise rhythm in spoken words.
- Continue a rhyming string.
- Hear and say the initial sound in words and know which letters represent some of the sounds.

### Early learning goals

- Hear and say sounds in words in the order in which they occur.
- Link sounds to letters, naming and sounding the letters of the alphabet.
- Use their phonic knowledge to write simple regular words and make phonetically plausible attempts at more complex words.

### Key words

rhyming, rhythmic, alliteration, awareness, recognise, hear and say, sounds

# Main story: *The Gruffalo*
## (Julia Donaldson and Axel Schaffer (1999), Macmillan, Basingstoke)

The Big Book version is ideal to use with the following activities. The Gruffalo tells the tale of the little mouse who lives in the forest and who calmly tricks Fox, Owl and Snake, three animals who would really like to eat him, about the mysterious and fierce monster called the Gruffalo. Does the Gruffalo really exist, do we wonder? Be assured, for a little creature, the mouse is extremely clever! Find out what happens when he finally does meet the Gruffalo.

## Activities

- Read the story using three storytellers: one person takes on the voice of the narrator, one the mouse and the other takes on the voice of Fox, Owl, Snake and the Gruffalo. Alternatively two people can read the story effectively, with one person taking on the voice of the narrator and the mouse and the other Fox, Owl, Snake and the Gruffalo. Both ways are successful.

- Remember to read the preface to the book first before you turn to the main story to give children a clue as to what it is about and to engage their interest.

- Make sure you read with clear intonation, with expression, and rhythmically.

- Ask the children what they notice about the story (it is told in rhyme). Read some of the rhyming couplets and ask the children to identify the rhyming pairs or the words that sound similar. Make a list with the children.

- Introduce the concept of alliteration using the children's names, for example 'Happy Hamid', 'Smiley Sarah'. (It is probably a good idea to work out one alliterative phrase per child to enable pace of input. Do value the children's own ideas however if they come up with their own suggestions.) This activity will also provide an opportunity to draw children's attention to initial letter sounds. Model the sounds for the children and ask them to repeat.

- Extend the concept of initial-letter sounds using a good selection of alphabet books, including alphabet books from different cultures.

- Use the text to extend the concept of alliteration. There are many examples, such as 'deep dark wood', terrible tusks', 'terrible teeth', 'knobbly knees', 'turned-out toes', 'purple prickles.' Extend the two-word phrases into three-word phrases with the children: for example, 'deep, dingy, dark wood', 'two terrible tusks'. Encourage the children to create their own two- and three-word alliterative phrases using the same initial letter sounds.

- Write a class poem describing the Gruffalo using the children's own words. Choose a portion of the text in which the descriptive words need to be filled in. Spell simple CVC (consonant, vowel, consonant) and CVCC words with the children, segmenting the sounds from the start of the word to the end (i.e. from left to right), building on their existing phonic knowledge. A similar approach would be to write alternative versions of familiar nursery rhymes.

- The book now comes with a CD. Put it on for the children to listen to independently in the listening corner, with copies of the text for them to follow.

- Look for alliteration in other rhymes and stories.

## Key questions

- What do you think this book is going to be about?

- Why?

- What makes you say that?

- Why do you think this is the Gruffalo? (Looking at the book cover.) Could the mouse be the Gruffalo? Why not?

- What do you think will happen next?

- How did the mouse trick the Gruffalo?

- Which two words sound similar?

- What sound(s) can you hear?

- What sound can you hear at the beginning of your name?

- Which sound can you hear next?

## Look, listen and note

Record children's progress in terms of their phonic knowledge; the beginnings of their ability to decode text.

## Effective practice

Set activities in meaningful contexts such as using the children's names as a starting point to look at initial-letter sounds.

## Planning and resourcing

Familiarise yourself with the guidance on the EYFS CD-ROM (Learning and Development/Communication, Language and Literacy/Early Reading) and Phases 1, 2 and 3 of Letters and Sounds.

## Home links

Make sure that parents and carers know the setting policy linking sounds and letters. It may be beneficial to run a workshop introducing them in particular to Phases 1 and 2 of Letters and Sounds (or the synthetic phonics programme that you use), as well as showing how you incorporate letters and sounds as part of children's everyday play. If parents and carers can understand the rationale behind the synthetic phonics approach, they can support their children at home. Do emphasise that simply enjoying sharing stories together is one of the best things they can do with their children. Children must view looking at story books together as a pleasurable experience, not merely an excuse for another decoding exercise. The emphasis must be on approaching story books with a view to engagement with and enjoyment of the text.

## *Additional resources*

There are many alphabet books available. Here are just a few:

- Hughes, Shirley (1997) *Alfie's Alphabet,* London: Red Fox. Alfie and his younger sister Annie Rose are familiar characters to many children. They will be able to identify with the familiar vocabulary and scenes from this book.

- Onyefulu, Ifeoma (1993) *A is for Africa,* London: Frances Lincoln. A well known, timeless, multicultural alphabet book.

- Alys-Browne, Philippa (1995) *African Animals ABC,* Bath: Barefoot Books. A beautifully illustrated book; each page depicts the animal featured engaged in a typical activity. The book uses simple, rhyming text. At the end of the book there are notes by the author providing information for older children and adults on the habitat and behaviour patterns of the animals.

- Zephaniah, Benjamin and Das, Prodeepta (2006) *J is for Jamaica,* London: Frances Lincoln. This alphabet book introduces children to the Caribbean island of Jamaica, exploring some of its sights, tastes and sounds.

In addition, the Early Learning Centre (www.elc.co.uk) do a lift-out alphabet puzzle, and an Alligator Alphabet Floor Puzzle is available from Barefoot Books (www.barefootbooks-online.co.uk).

## Rhyming story books

- Alborough, Jez (2002) *Where's My Teddy!* London: Walker Books. Brilliant, humorous tale of Eddy who has lost his teddy in the deep, dark wood ... He finds a bear, but not the bear he is looking for!

(♪) Andreae, Giles and Parker-Rees, Guy (2000) *Giraffes Can't Dance,* London: Orchard Picturebooks. The story of Gerald the giraffe who was not a good dancer and who dreaded the yearly Jungle Dance. However, this year, Gerald finds a different song to dance to, one that suits him, with heart-warming consequences!

(♪) Freedman, Claire and Cort, Ben (2007) *Aliens Love Underpants,* London: Simon & Schuster. Children will find this book extremely funny. It is all about aliens who are not interested in human beings at all when they fly down to Earth, but merely want their underpants instead. This story will make sure children want to wear clean underwear for life!

(♪) Sharratt, Nick and Tucker, Stephen (2004) *Goldilocks,* Basingstoke: Macmillan. Delightful, funky version of the traditional tale retold completely in rhyme. Great fun!

## The EYFS principles

The activities related to the Gruffalo rhyme allow for individual responses to the text. Children are able to develop their knowledge of linking letters and sounds in a supportive, no-risk environment which enables them to develop at their own pace.

# 4 | Reading

**From birth–20 months**

## Development matters

- Listen to familiar sounds, words, or finger plays.
- Respond to words and interactive rhymes, such as 'Clap Hands'.

## Key words
listen, respond, familiar, interactive

## Main story: *Clap Hands, Baby*
**(Claire Henley (illustrator) (2006), Penguin, London)**

Book and CD that aim to stimulate the minds and senses of babies. The book is about experiences and noises that will be familiar to babies, such as the 'choo choo' of a toy train from the toy basket, or the 'clickety-clack' of a shape sorter. The CD contains a delightful selection of rhymes to sing and dance along to. Children sing most of the rhymes, and a song sheet is included. Children will love *Clap Hands:* the book, CD and song sheet come in a zipped carry case with a strap that will appeal very much.

## Activities

- Familiarise yourself with the content of the book and CD.

- Begin to learn the rhymes and songs included.

- Share with babies, modelling the actions and singing at the same time.

- As babies become familiar with the content, concentrate on favourite rhymes and songs from the CD, encouraging them to make a response as you maintain eye contact with them, and smile.

- Provide as many of the toys featured in the book as you can so that babies and toddlers can hear the noises that they make.

### Key questions

- Can you sing with me?

- Can you say it with me?

- Where are your hands?

- Can you clap your hands like this?

- Which is your favourite rhyme?

- Are you ready?

- What noise does it make?

## Look, listen and note

Note children's responses to the games you play with them and the stories that you read.

## Effective practice

Use finger play as part of your non-verbal communication with babies to support eye contact and engagement as you sing or tell rhymes such as 'Two Little Dicky Birds.' Encourage children to join in.

## Planning and resourcing

- Develop a library of books specifically to use with babies; they do respond from a very early age.

- Include CDs of rhymes and stories to use within the setting.

## Home links

Communicate with parents and carers about familiar songs and rhymes from home. Learn them so that you can incorporate favourites within the setting with the children.

## Additional resources

You will be able to find most of the toys featured in the book from the Early Learning Centre (www.elc.co.uk). You will also find a Fisher Price child's CD player at www.fisher-price.com.

You might like to revisit some of the Additional Resources listed in Chapter 3 for the age group 'From Birth–20 months', such as *Action Songs and Rhymes for Babies and Toddlers* by Sheena Roberts. You could also look at *This Little Puffin Finger Plays and Nursery Rhymes* by Elizabeth Matterson and Claudia Munoz, featured in Chapter 3 (From birth–20 months).

(♪)  Land, Fiona (2007) *Baby Touch Rhyme Book,* London: Ladybird. Tactile, interactive rhyme book full of well-known rhymes to sing together.

## ⬡⬡ The EYFS principles

The above suggestions support children as individuals through allowing plenty of choice for babies and toddlers to choose and respond to favourite rhymes and songs as these become familiar to them.

## From 16–36 months

### Development matters

- Show interest in stories, songs and rhymes.

- Have some favourite stories, rhymes, songs, poems or jingles.

### Key words
interest, favourite, stories, songs, rhymes

## Main story: *Clap Your Hands*
**(David Ellwand (2002), Handprint Books, New York)**

Exciting and well-illustrated board book which depicts groups of teddies doing the actions to the familiar rhyme, 'If You're Happy and You Know It.' This comforting and reassuring book will appeal to children of this age, providing a familiar context as they will all have teddies or other favourite soft toys at home.

## Activities

- Sing the familiar rhyme with the children using the book to illustrate the actions.

- If you have enough teddy bears at your setting hand them out to small groups of children; alternatively, invite them to bring in their own. Sing the rhyme together and encourage the children to make their teddy bears do the actions. Model the idea for them using a teddy bear of your own.

- Sing the rhyme again, copying the actions of the teddy bears in the book and encouraging the children to join in. This is a rhyme that can be sung outdoors as well as indoors.

- Read lots of stories and rhymes about teddy bears with the children (see Additional Resources).

- Make simple teddy-bear puppets with the children to use when telling the stories and singing the rhymes. Stuff two felt teddy-bear shapes with filling, and glue the shapes together with PVC glue. Stick on eyes, a nose and a mouth.

### Key questions

- Where are the teddies?

- What are they doing?

- What do you think they are going to do next?

- Can you show me how you clap your hands, touch your toes, etc.?

- Can you make your teddy bears clap their hands, touch their toes, etc.?

## Look, listen and note

- Note children's responses to the stories you read with them. Discover their interests and find appropriate stories for them to engage with.

- Which books and stories do the children return to independently?

## Effective practice

- Use visual aids to support your storytelling techniques such as puppets, soft toys and real objects.

- Find stories that relate to children's real-life experiences so that they can draw on book language to extend their own vocabulary.

## Planning and resourcing

Where possible, include dual language texts to match the languages spoken by families in your setting library.

## Home links

- Ensure that your setting runs an efficient book-lending scheme so that books are going home with children on a regular basis.

- Hand out a leaflet with local library information on it, including opening times.

- Find out whether there are any storytelling sessions in your local area and always keep parents and carers informed of these.

## Additional resources

You might like to revisit some of the Additional Resources listed in Chapter 3 for the age range 'From 30–60+ months' for other stories told in rhyme.

📖 Kennedy, Jimmy and Theobalds, Prue, *The Teddy Bears' Picnic,* Uplands Books. An excellent story book version of the traditional song that children will love to sing along to.

📖 Alborough, Jez (2006) *Where's My Teddy! Listen and Join In!* London: Walker Books. A mixed-media pack that includes a mini-hardback edition of *Where's My Teddy?* and a CD which features very funny readings of *Where's My Teddy? It's the Bear* and *My Friend Bear* as well as songs and suggestions for story-based activities. Excellent value pack.

📖 Alborough, Jez (2004) *It's the Bear,* London: Walker Books. Eddy is going for a picnic in the woods with his mum, but he knows there is a bear who lives in there. Will Eddy become a picnic for the bear?

📖 Alborough, Jez (2004) *My Friend Bear,* London: Walker Books. Eddy and the bear both feel sad and wish they had a friend to talk to. They both have their teddies with them, and they both know that teddies cannot talk – oh really?!

## The EYFS principles

The above activities respond to individual needs and develop children's engagement with texts at a very early age. Supporting an environment in which stories and rhymes are an integral part of everyday practice will enable children to approach texts with eagerness as they begin to make a logical progression towards the specifics of decoding the written word for themselves.

# From 30–60+ months

## Development matters

- Listen to and join in with stories and poems, one to one and also in small groups.

- Begin to be aware of the way stories are structured.

- Suggest how the story might end.

- Show interest in illustrations and print in books and print in the environment.

- Handle books carefully.

- Know information can be relayed in the form of print.

- Hold books the correct way up and turn pages.

- Understand the concept of a word.

- Enjoy an increasing range of books.

- Know that information can be retrieved from books and computers.

## Early learning goals

- Explore and experiment with sounds, words and texts.

- Retell narratives in the correct sequence, drawing on language patterns of stories.

- Read a range of familiar and common words and simple sentences independently.

- Know that print carries meaning and, in English, is read from left to right and top to bottom.

- Show an understanding of the elements of stories, such as main character, sequence of events and openings, and how information can be found in non-fiction texts to answer questions about where, who, why and how.

## Key words

listen, join in, story (structure, ending, language patterns of, elements), retell, read, explore, experiment

# Main story: *The Very Hungry Caterpillar*
## (Eric Carle (1994), Puffin Books, London)

The Big-Book version would be ideal for some of the following activities. Classic tale of the tiny caterpillar who spends a whole week eating increasing amounts of fruit before eating far too much of the 'wrong' kind of food on Saturday. He eats something far better for him on Sunday. The story reveals how he eventually becomes a beautiful butterfly. The book will support children's understanding of healthy eating, of numbers and days of the week, as well as introducing the life cycle of a butterfly.

## Activities

- Use a story sack to tell the tale of the Very Hungry Caterpillar.

- The tale also lends itself well to storyboarding.

- Visual aids such as those from a story sack act as clues or prompts which support children to retell the story. *The Very Hungry Caterpillar* is a good story to use to support an activity such as retelling the narrative because it incorporates the days of the week and counting, giving it a clear, meaningful sequence for young children and a definite structure to which they can respond positively. Use the story sack or the storyboard resources on the carpet area of the setting or on the talk table, or even outdoors if you have an appropriate area, to support a fun way of inviting children to retell the familiar tale. The book has one main character so is also good for introducing children to this concept for the first time.

- As children retell the story, have the text available. Point to the words to draw attention to the text as they retell the tale supported by the visual aids.

- If they show interest in the written words, use the opportunity to talk to them about the narrative. Ask them where the words are and where you start reading from, for example.

- With children at the top end of the age range, encourage them to begin to decode the text independently; model blending individual sounds with them and following individual words from left to right as you read.

- Be specific with book language. Talk about the beginning and the end of the story.

- Make the most of the opportunity to talk about healthy eating!

- The book is an excellent way in to a topic on life cycles and can be supported by having butterflies hatch in the setting.

- Support the storytelling activities with a selection of related non-fiction texts.

## Key questions

- Can you tell me the story?

- Where are the words?

- Where do I start reading?

- What happens at the beginning of the story?

- What happens at the end of the story?

- What is the next word?

- Do you know what this word says?

- What is the first sound?

## Look, listen and note

- Note which stories and poems children return to regularly when in the setting and ask them to retell them to you. Record the words and phrases they use, especially the story language they repeat. What phonic skills and reading strategies are they using when they approach a text?

- Note any words the children recognise, beginning with their own name.

- Note how the children approach books; do they hold them the right way round, do they turn the pages one at a time, do they know where the words are, for example.

- In addition, note children's approach to information texts. Do they know the purpose of information texts?

## Effective practice

- Support children's interests in books.

- Model appropriate book behaviour, including how to find out information from information texts.

## Planning and resourcing

- Develop a good selection of story sacks in your setting to support storytelling activities. (NB: it is much cheaper to make your own than to buy commercially.) Remember to include traditional tales and multicultural tales as part of the collection.

- Allow story sacks to go home with the children. Invite parents and carers to take part in a story sack workshop so that they know how to use them supportively with their children.

- Give books high priority; your setting needs an attractive book corner for the children to use. Go in there regularly and read with them on an informal basis.

## Home links

- Give parents and carers information on how to use story sacks with their children at home.

- Ask parents and carers to develop story sacks for the setting. Set a budget.

- Invite parents and carers to come in and read with the children during sessions. Include bilingual parents and carers and encourage them to read in their home language with their children.

## Additional resources

Go to www.sparklebox.co.uk/cdroms/srcd1 to find details of a CD-ROM incorporating ten sets of story visual aids, including a set for 'The Very Hungry Caterpillar.' One of the aids is a set of cards (11 centimetres square) for use with a Pixie programmable robot. Each story set can be bought individually if you would prefer.

- Hunter, Barbara (2003) *Life as a Butterfly*, London: Heinemann Educational Books. Information book especially designed for young learners depicting the life cycle of the butterfly and introducing the concept of change over time.

- Jarrett, Clare (2008) *Arabella Miller's Tiny Caterpillar*, London: Walker Books Ltd. Arabella makes friends with a tiny caterpillar and must wait patiently for a wonderful secret to be revealed … Use this book in conjunction with teaching children the rhyme Little Arabella Miller:

*Little Arabella Miller*
*Found a hairy caterpillar.*
*First it crawled upon her mother;*
*Then upon her baby brother.*
*All said, 'Arabella Miller,*
*Take away that caterpillar!'*

## Alternative story titles

📖 Murphy, Jill (1983) *Whatever Next!* London: Pan Macmillan. Wonderful fantasy tale of Baby Bear who finds a cardboard box for a rocket, Wellingtons for space boots and a colander for a helmet before flying to the moon. He has a picnic with an owl and still manages to get back home before bath time! A story to spark children's imaginations. What exciting adventure could they have between tea and bath time?

📖 Gray, Kes and Parsons, Garry (2004) *Billy's Bucket,* London: Red Fox. The cautionary tale of Billy, who sets great store by the bucket he chooses for his birthday. Nobody believes the amazing things that Billy has in his bucket. His insistence that no one can borrow his bucket goes unheeded by his parents, and the story ends with disastrous consequences! Another tale that will spark children's imaginations – why would nobody be able to borrow their bucket?

# The EYFS principles

The above activities respond to the fact that children arrive at early childhood settings at different stages with regard to reading development. Whilst there is a regularity that characterises reading development, children reach developmental landmarks through a variety of different routes shaped by personal, social and cultural factors. Children must therefore be treated as unique individuals in this respect, and the environment should be structured so as to enable their individual reading development.

# 5 | Writing

## Development matters

- Move arms and legs and increasingly use them to reach for, grasp and manipulate things.

- Begin to make marks.

## Key words
reach, grasp, make marks

## Main story: *Kipper's Toybox*
(Mick Inkpen (1993), Hodder & Stoughton, London)

This is the story of Kipper the dog who has trouble counting his toys one day: then he realises that something, or someone, has been nibbling a hole in his toy box. Even worse, Sock Thing has gone missing. Kipper hears strange noises in the middle of the night and sees Sock Thing wriggling across the floor! Then Kipper makes a strange discovery involving two tiny mice and solves the mystery of both his missing toy and the hole in his toy box.

## Activities

Although not a 'baby book' per se, there are still many opportunities to use this text to develop babies' gross motor skills using a combination of visual aids and your own personal knowledge of the story. The story is best told using resources from a story sack. A group of very kind parents made the one I used to use in the nursery where I taught. It is one of the easier story sacks to make. Learn the story off by heart, because you can adapt it by creating a simpler version for young babies.

- With babies, retell the story simply, placing the toys around them within reaching distance.

  - Encourage them to reach for, touch and hold on to the toys and talk about their properties: the slipper will be soft, for example and can be stroked. Babies can do this on their tummies and then as they learn to sit up independently.

  - Call the toys by the names in the book: Big Owl, Hippopotamus, Slipper, Rabbit, Mr Snake and Sock Thing.

  - Make sure the resources you use or make are suitable for children under the age of three years. You might also want to make sure they are machine washable as children this age will put everything in their mouths.

- Read the story to the children, either on a one-to-one or small-group basis and model reaching for or holding on to the appropriate toys, picking them up and putting them down as required at each stage of the story.

- As children become older, and are secure on their feet, place all the toys on a blanket on the floor. Read the story from the text and invite the children to find the appropriate toys for you.

- Leave the toys in the story sack. Can the children find them in there for you? The story sack will seem huge and will really encourage them to reach and grasp. Hold the top of the sack open for them to support them and give them reassurance that it is 'safe to go in there'.

- Add a toy box (simply a large cardboard box). Encourage the children to find the toys as you read the story and to put them in and take them out of the toy box.

- Make a hole in the toy box, big enough for some of the toys to fall out from when you lift it up. Have fun with the children with this. Ask them to pick up the toys for you and put them back in the box. As they put them back in, others will fall out!

- Leave the visual aids and the toy box out for the children to access independently. What do they do with them?

- Encourage mark-making using the media of paint. Create paintings of Kipper and his toys using large paintbrushes.

## Key questions

- Can you find it?

- Where is it?

- Can you reach it?

- Can you hold it?

- What does it feel like?

- Which toy are we looking for?

- Who have you painted?

### Look, listen and note

Are children's coordinated movements progressing and developing as they should? Seek advice if you are at all unsure from a senior practitioner.

## Effective practice

Talk with the children about which of Kipper's toys they have painted. Always ask them what any marks they make represent.

## Planning and resourcing

- Use a variety of mark-making materials for children to experiment with in the setting: crayons, felt-tip pens, play-dough cutters, clay tools, chalk, etc.

- Include experiences such as making marks using their hands such as in shaving foam and gloop.

- If children show a preference for a particular medium, give them the opportunity to use it again and again.

## Home links

- Make sure your allergy information from home is up-to-date if you decide to use substances such as shaving foam in your setting. Some children may have to use protective gloves.

- Talk with parents and carers about the reaching and grasping movements their children are capable of making to encourage them to incorporate opportunities at home to support their development and coordination.

- Make sure that parents and carers understand how their child's physical development (e.g., learning to reach for toys and throwing a ball) benefits early writing skills through developing hand–eye coordination.

## Additional resources

As you develop an awareness of children's favourite stories, songs and rhymes, ensure you incorporate the use of simple visual aids as you read and sing together, especially soft toys, which are appealing for very young children to reach, grasp and touch. Look at some of the choices in Additional Resources for this age group in previous chapters for further ideas. Look out for additional titles on the same character. For those children who become fans of Kipper, for example, there are now many more titles to choose from, including *Kipper's Story Collection* by Mick Inkpen, which contains four Kipper stories ('Kipper', 'Kipper's Birthday', 'Kipper's Toybox' and 'Kipper's Snowy Day') and is again published by Hachette Children's Books.

Puppets by Post (www.puppetsbypost.com) does an amazing 'Mice in a Red Box' puppet which works with three fingers underneath: the mice gently push their way out to see what they can see! This is perfect to use with Three Blind Mice, for example. They also do a selection of story books with puppets, many of which are used or listed within this book.

## The EYFS principles

- The above activities based on the suggested text support each child as a unique individual.

- The environment, in the form of appropriate resources, enables children's learning and development through giving opportunities for the early stages of writing to form whilst at the same time allowing each child to develop at their own pace and according to their own particular interests.

# From 16–36 months

## Main story: *The Very Busy Spider*
**(Eric Carle (1996), Puffin Books, London)**

This is the story of a spider who lives on a farm. She creates her web as the story is told. She is very busy spinning her web and cannot stop when some of the animals invite her to do other things like 'run in the meadow' and 'roll in the mud'. Finally, the web is finished. The rooster comes by chasing a 'pesty fly' and asks the spider if she wants to catch it. The spider does catch it; in her newly made web! Use the board-book version for the following activities. It provides a sensory experience for children because the spider's web is raised and they can trace it with their finger.

## Activities

- Familiarise children with the story. Allow them to trace the raised spider's web in the book.

- Use silver metallic pens and black paper for the children to create their own spider webs, either with support or independently.

- Create raised spider webs using glue pens and silver glitter. Children will have to create a complete web pattern with the glue pens before they add any glitter, so do model this activity for them so that they are sure about what they need to do before they have a go. Encourage the children to trace over the patterns they make when the webs are dry.

- Encourage children to start to write their names on their work. Treat them as able writers. Encourage them to use their name cards for support.

- Leave out metallic pens, crayons and paints (with a variety of thick and thin paintbrushes) for the children to access independently to make marks with. Talk with them about the marks they make.

### Key questions

- How did you make your spider web?

- Have you written your name on your spider web?

- What could you use to help you? (Name card)

- What have you written here?

- What would you like to use to write with?

## Look, listen and note

What children say about the marks they make. If they ascribe meaning to those marks, write it down. If they describe a painting or drawing to you, such as the spider webs, write down the language that they use.

## Effective practice

- Provide opportunities for children to experiment with mark-making.

- Draw children's attention to print around them. Include scripts from all the languages represented in the setting so that children understand that meaning is universally conveyed by print.

## Planning and resourcing

- Make sure there are plentiful opportunities in the setting for children to experiment with mark-making.

- Make sure children observe you writing in the setting.

- Develop a collection of resources displaying scripts relevant for all children in the setting, including dual-language books, food labels, posters and fabric shopping bags.

## Home links

- Ask parents and carers to donate resources to the setting from their language communities.

- Host an early writing workshop for parents and carers so that they understand that mark-making is an important phase of their children's journey into conventional writing. Encourage them to talk with their children about the marks they make at home.

## Additional resources

Look in your setting's educational resource catalogues for metallic crayons, pens and paint. If you are having difficulty finding these, a set of Crayola metallic crayons in gold, silver and bronze can be purchased from www.artastik.co.uk. S and S Services (www.ss-services.co.uk) specialises in early years resources and stocks metallic paint, gold and silver ink pens and Crayola metallic markers in packs of five.

### Alternative story titles

Child, Lauren (2005) *But Excuse Me That Is My Book*, London: Puffin. Not everyone is a fan of Lola; however, this is a great book about children and their relationship with books, especially favourite books. It opens children's eyes to the fact that there is a book to be found on just about anything they want to read or find out about. Lola's favourite book at the moment is *Beetles, Bugs and Butterflies*. This story could lead into activities relating to children writing about their own favourite books. A scribing activity could be done on a one-to-one basis – for example, building on children's language for communication and thinking skills.

Allen, Jonathan (1997) *Chicken Licken,* London: Picture Corgi Books. A great lift-the-flap version of the story of Chicken Licken who thinks the sky is falling down when an acorn falls on his head and he must go and tell the King. Create maps of Chicken Licken's journey with the children, encouraging them to use their mark-making skills to label characters and landmarks along the way.

# The EYFS principles

The above approach recognises that each child makes his or her own individual journey into conventional writing and that the early stages of mark-making are an extremely important phase. Each child will develop personal preferences which can be supported in the setting through the development of appropriate resources.

# From 30–60+ months

## Development matters

- Sometimes give meaning to marks as they draw and paint.

- Ascribe meanings to marks that they see in different places.

- Begin to break the flow of speech into words.

- Use writing as a means of recording and communicating.

## Early learning goals

- Use their phonic knowledge to write simple regular words and make phonetically plausible attempts at more complex words.

- Attempt writing for different purposes, using features of different forms such as lists, stories and instructions.

- Write their own names and other things such as labels and captions and begin to form simple sentences, sometimes using punctuation.

## Key words

ascribe meaning to marks, writing, recording, communicating

# Main story: *Miranda the Castaway*
**(James Mayhew (1997), Orion Children's Books, London)**

This is the story of a little girl called Miranda. Miranda has been shipwrecked on a desert island. How is she going to survive? At first she is unsure of what to do but then she becomes extremely innovative and slowly creates a life for herself on the island, including building a house of her own. As time passes, she becomes more and more comfortable on the island and even plants seeds and grows flowers in her garden. Her house becomes bigger with a bedroom, kitchen, bathroom and a toilet! Miranda becomes lonely, however, and her biggest challenge of all is to work out a way to get home ...

## Activities

- Read the story with the children. This is a very exciting story, full of surprises, so make sure you are familiar with it yourself before you share it. You will then be able to read with intonation to bring it alive and also ask appropriate open-ended questions regarding the content.

- The story could easily be linked in with an overall topic on pirates, ships or the sea.

- Make maps of the island with the children, either A3 or A4 size.

  - Model creating a map with them and explain what a landmark is.

  - The maps could be stained using a tea bag to make them look old (stain them before the children write on them); I have even torn around the edges slightly with children to make them look old. This works especially well if you are thinking along the lines of a pirate or ships theme. Let the children use charcoal or thick black felt-tip pens for authenticity to write landmarks or mark-make on the maps in this case.

  - Alternatively, use plain white paper and coloured felt-tip pens or colouring pencils.

  - Encourage the children to write on landmarks, or scribe the words for them.

  - Support their efforts at writing, especially children nearer the top end of the age range in relation to their developing phonic knowledge.

- Write rescue letters from Miranda to put in bottles to 'throw' into the sea. Make sure the bottles are completely dry before you put the letters in.

- Model the conventions of letter-writing during a shared write with children at the top end of the age range. Scribe the letters for younger children, but do encourage them to write their own name at the end.

- Create a role-play area of Miranda's island home. Put paper and writing implements in there so that the children can draw their own maps and write their own rescue messages independently.

- Put resources such as a pirate ship in the sand tray and shells, sharks and turtles in the water tray to create language opportunities for the children in relation to the topic or story.

- Design an island home for Miranda. Encourage the children to use their emergent writing skills to label their designs. Use junk modelling materials to create the designed homes.

- Rewrite the end of the story with the children. Talk about how else she could have left the island. Encourage children at the top end of the age range to write their own endings.

## Key questions

- What do you think this book is going to be about?

- What makes you say that?

- How does Miranda feel now?

- How would you feel if you were shipwrecked on a desert island?

- What will she do next?

- What else could she have done?

- Which landmarks have you drawn on your map?

- What have you written here?

- How does your story end?

- What is the first sound you can hear?

- Which sound can you hear next?

## Look, listen and note

- Note children's approach to writing:

- Do they perceive their developing skills as meaningful communication?

- Are they making use of their developing phonic knowledge to attempt to spell words and simple sentences?

## Effective practice

Support children as they develop their ability to hear the sounds in words in the order in which they occur from beginning to end. When you act as scribe for the children, model this approach to spelling with them.

## Planning and resourcing

- Provide plenty of opportunities for writing in the setting, including independently.

- Develop a bank of phonics resources to support children's developing blending and segmenting skills.

## Home links

- Make sure parents and carers understand the difference between blending phonemes for reading and segmenting phonemes for writing.

- Encourage parents and carers to provide writing opportunities at home and to share with you their child's early attempts to communicate meaningfully on paper. Show them examples of what they have been doing in the setting.

- Ensure parents and carers are aware of displays in the setting that incorporate the children's writing so that they can see that their child's writing progress is typical of their age.

## Additional resources

Wallace, John (2002) *Pirate Boy,* London: HarperCollins. Another story with a very smart child as the central character. Pirate Boy lives on a ship with two wicked pirates and is treated badly, so he escapes with their boat to a deserted island. The pirates are cross, however, and set out to find him. Pirate Boy has to think of a way to outwit them somehow …

Cole, Babette (1995) *The Bad Good Manners Book,* London: Puffin. Appealing and very funny book about how to behave. The illustrations are brilliant and support the text perfectly. Children will love this book. Encourage them to write their own lists of 'bad good manners'!

Allen, Jonathan (1997) *Chicken Licken,* London: Picture Corgi. A great lift-the-flap version of the story of Chicken Licken who thinks the sky is falling down when an acorn falls on his head and he must go and tell the King. This text is also listed in the Additional Resources for the previous age range in this chapter. The book provides a great, humorous introduction to speech bubbles.

Allen, Nicholas (2000) *The Queens Knickers,* London: Red Fox. Fabulous story of the different types of underwear the Queen must wear on every occasion, from a garden party to the opening of Parliament to which she must wear her VIP knickers (Very Important Pair). Invite children to design a pair of knickers for the Queen and display along with instructions as to which occasion she must wear them to and why.

# ⬡⬡ The EYFS principles

It is important to treat children as competent learners from birth. Treating children as writers very early on will:

1   draw their awareness to the functions of print;

2   support their perceptions of themselves as capable of communicating meaningfully through early mark making to their earliest attempts to reproduce letters and words.

# Handwriting

 **From birth–20 months**

> ### Development matters
>
> - Play with own fingers and toes and focus on objects around them.
> - Begin to bring together hand and eye movements to fix on and make contact with objects.
>
> ### Key words
> play, fingers, toes, objects, focus, hand–eye coordination

## Main story: *Jack-in-the-box from Oranges and Lemons*
**(Karen King and Ian Beck (2006), Oxford University Press, Oxford)**

This nursery song is one of a collection of twenty illustrated action songs. The book also includes the music for each song.

*Jack-in-the-box …*
*Jumps up like this!*
*He makes me laugh as he waggles his head.*
*I gently press him down again,*
*Saying: 'Jack-in-the-box,*
*You must go to bed.'*

## Activities

- Use a simple Jack-in-the-box toy as you sing the song with babies to engage their attention.

- Encourage them to watch the toy.

- Model how to play with it to release the Jack-in-the-box.

- As children become older, for example once they are capable of sitting independently, let them play with the toy for themselves and try and release the Jack-in-the-box.

- Develop the song in relation to the suggested actions in the book as children become slightly older and more stable on their feet.

### Key questions

- What's going to happen?

- Can you see him? (When Jack pops up.)

- Where did he come from?

- Where did he go? (When you put Jack back in the box.)

- When will he jump up again do you think?

- How can you make Jack jump up?

## Look, listen and note

- How young babies focus on objects around them.

- Which objects or toys they find attractive and enjoy playing with.

- How do they indicate what they want to play with?

- What movements and sounds do they make?

## Effective practice

- Place toys within easy reach of young babies who cannot sit up independently, such as attached to the side of a cot.

- Describe the movements they need to make in order to manipulate toys as they play and experiment with them such as, 'I can see that you are pushing the button to make the music play.'

## Planning and resourcing

- Provide plenty of toys for babies to reach and grasp with their arms and legs, such as a baby gym.

- Keep planning activities to develop gross and fine motor skills.

- Develop a repertoire of favourite action songs to sing with the children.

## Home links

- Find out which songs and rhymes parents and carers sing at home with their children and use some of these as part of daily practice.

- Send home copies of favourite songs and rhymes with actions for parents and carers to use at home with their children. Whilst most parents and carers interact naturally with their children, there are many who will be grateful for advice and support in relation to their child's physical and educational development.

- Discover favourite toys that babies and young children enjoy at home. Is it possible to provide similar toys in the setting?

## The EYFS principles

The simple activities described above recognise the importance of the gradual refinement of hand–eye coordination from birth so that children will eventually be able to manipulate smaller objects with a view to developing a viable handwriting style.

## From 16–36 months

### Development matters

- Make random marks with their fingers and some tools.

- Begin to show some control in their use of tools and equipment.

### Key words
make random marks, fingers, tools, control

## Main story: *Handa's Surprise*
**(Eileen Browne (1995), Walker Books, London)**

The story of Handa who one day decides to take 'seven delicious fruits' to her friend Akeyo. As she makes her way to Akeyo's village, the illustrations in the book depict a wonderful subtext for the reader who can see each of the fruits being pinched by several animals along the way. In the meantime, Handa, who has no idea about what is happening, muses about which fruit Akeyo will like best. The basket empties, but Handa surprisingly arrives at Akeyo's village with a basket full of tangerines! How could this possibly have happened? Only the reader will be able to solve the mystery! A fantastic multicultural tale. Handa is from the Luo tribe of south-west Kenya.

## Activities

- Create a large desert background with the children using the book illustrations as your starting point. Use paint and rollers and brushes of different thicknesses. Mix flour with the paint for a textured, 3-D effect.

- Ask the children to look at and point out the colours in the book illustrations.

- Provide appropriate coloured paints; however, white could be included amongst your selection to provide opportunities to experiment with mixing lighter shades. Model using directional brush strokes for the grass, painting from the top of the grass to the bottom.

- Encourage children to use their fingers to create the insects that fly around Handa's fruit.

- Make the background large enough to cover a display board. The children can then paint the animals that took Handa's fruit on the background once it is dry.

- Alternatively, weave the desert background. Use garden netting and strips of blue, yellow, brown and green material. Make sure you choose a large enough space in the classroom on which to work successfully – weaving is hard work for children this age and they will need to be able to move around. Use a square table without chairs, for example or get down on the floor. Weave a couple of lines yourself to give the children an example to follow. If you weave from left to right you will be emulating the directionality of writing in English.

- Leave another piece of large netting or smaller pieces for individual work with pieces of material for the children to access independently.

- Make clay animals from the story and the different pieces of fruit. Provide clay tools so that the children can create facial features for the animals, for example. Encourage problem-solving. How could they create the effect of the monkey's fur/the texture of the pineapple, for example? If you are making fruit, put all the seven fruits in a basket for the children to observe and touch.

- Turn your role play corner into Handa's home. Include items such as a broom to sweep the floor with and pots with wooden spoons for cooking. These are activities which will provide opportunities for fine and gross motor development, as well as hand–eye coordination.

- Develop a set of small-world play resources to use in the dry sand tray: the animals, the fruit, Handa and Akeyo, the desert trees.

- Retell the story with the children as they move the resources around to echo the text: the ostrich leaning into the basket to take the guava for example, or the parrot hanging upside down in the tree to take the passion fruit.

- Alternatively, put plastic (or real) fruit and a selection of baskets in the outside sand pit. Support children filling a basket with 'seven delicious fruits' and walking with it balanced on their head across the sand (it is probably a good idea to suggest that they use either one or two hands on either side of the basket. You could model how to do this).

- Model counting pieces of fruit using one-to-one ordination.

## Key questions

- What colours can you see in the illustration on the page?

- What colour paints will we need?

- How could you make that colour lighter?

- Which animal are you painting?

- Are the strips of material the same colours as the ones in the book?

- What happens next in the story?

- What is happening now?

- Who takes the banana, guava, mango?

- How many fruits do you have in your basket?

## Look, listen and note

- Note the way children use the equipment you provide.

- Look at whether they have any control over the tools they are using, which tools they prefer to mark make with and what kinds of mark they prefer to make.

- Explore the meaning of some of the marks they make independently.

## Effective practice

Encourage children to use the resources you provide to develop their manipulative skills. Model using them alongside the children.

## Planning and resourcing

- Provide a wide range of resources to develop children's fine and gross motor skills.

- Plan activities that specifically target the development of children's fine and gross motor skills.

## Home links

Talk to parents and carers about work the children produce in the set-ting and their mark-making skills. Raise parents' and carers' awareness of the fact that the marks children produce on the page always occur within the light of a specific context which supports the intentionality of those marks and gives them meaning. Sometimes the context is child-led, sometimes adult-led.

## Additional resources

There are plenty of story books that lend themselves to experimenting with paint and other media for backgrounds to displays, or for individual work. Here are a few suggestions, some of which have already been listed in previous chapters:

- Lacome, J. (1993) *Walking through the Jungle,* London: Walker Books. Excellent use of rhyme and simple repetitive language structures to depict the journey of a small child making his way through the jungle. He hears different jungle noises along the way, but the page must be turned to reveal the animal responsible for the noise. Use as the basis for creating a jungle background.

- Waddell, Martin and Oxenbury, Helen (1995) *Farmer Duck,* London: Walker Books. The story of a duck who has to do all the work on the farm by himself because he lives with a lazy farmer who spends all day in bed. Eventually, the other animals on the farm decide to do something about the situation. They chase the lazy farmer away and run the farm together! Provide lots of small-world role play opportunities for children based on this text.

- Cooper, Helen (1998) *Pumpkin Soup,* London: Random House Children's Books. The story of three good friends, Cat, Squirrel and Duck, who make the best pumpkin soup together every day. Unfortunately, Duck decides one day that he wants to be Head Cook, leading to all sorts of upset. The story does have a happy ending, reminding the reader what true friendship is all about.

Encourage children to write their own recipe for Pumpkin Soup. Provide a large cooking pot, possible ingredients and wooden spoons for the children to role play making the soup.

## The EYFS principles

The activities described above move forwards the ongoing refinement of hand–eye coordination from birth alongside the development of fine and gross motor skills so that children will eventually be able to manipulate smaller objects with precision and with a view to developing a viable handwriting style.

## From 30–60+ months

### Development matters

- Use one-handed tools and equipment.

- Draw lines and circles using gross motor movements.

- Manipulate objects with increasing control.

- Begin to use anticlockwise movement and retrace vertical lines.

- Begin to form recognisable letters.

### Early learning goals

- Use a pencil and hold it effectively to form recognisable letters, most of which are correctly formed.

### Key words

one-handed tools, draw lines and circles, manipulate, control, recognisable letters

# Main story: *The Kiss that Missed*
**(David Melling (2003), Hodder Children's Books, London)**

A classic 'Once upon a time' tale of the king who is too busy to give his son a royal kiss goodnight. Instead he blows one to him as he rushes past his bedroom door, but it misses him and escapes, bouncing 'out of the window and into the night'. Children must follow the knight on horseback as he tries to avoid danger in the wild wood on his journey to catch the kiss and bring it back to the palace. The knight rides through snow, past owls, and lurking wolves and bears. A tree trunk he finally rests on with his horse is not a tree trunk at all, but a very large, green dragon! The royal kiss is finally caught, but the dragon is in pursuit of the knight ... The story ends well, but provides lots of exciting tension, fun and drama to engage and inspire young minds. The story could be used as part of a general topic on castles.

## Activities

The activities below are designed to support and develop children's hand–eye coordination as well as their emergent writing skills.

- Develop the children's own versions of the kiss that missed. You could do this either on a one-to-one basis with younger children where you scribe their story for them, or as part of a shared write to model the conventions of story writing, particularly with children at the top end of this age range.

- Read lots of stories involving castles, princes and princesses (see Additional Resources below) so that children become immersed in the language of fairy tales, such as 'Once upon a time' and 'and they all lived happily ever after.'

- Make books for the children to write their story in. A very simple but effective A5 sized book can be made by using one or two pieces of A4 paper folded in half and placed inside a folded A4 coloured mount for the cover. Staple down the spine.

- Talk about the front cover and what needs to be included on it (the title, author, illustrator and perhaps the publisher).

- With younger children, encourage them to write their name independently either with or without the support of their name card.

- Encourage children to illustrate each page. Talk about their illustrations with them.

- Sew book marks using metallic thread for the children to use with their books.

- Leave empty books in the writing area for the children to access independently.

- Create 'Wanted' posters for the kiss that missed.

- Design a castle.

  - Talk about the features of a castle with the children first – make a list together.

  - Provide lots of visual support through non-fiction books and posters.

  - Making a list will give you another opportunity to model writing for the children and to focus on spelling, particularly with those from the top end of the age range.

  - Encourage the children to label their drawings independently, but do scribe for those who need your support in this way.

  - Build the castles from junk model materials. Create a display in the setting or classroom.

- Make royal jewellery; thread pasta (spray it gold!) or beads onto thread.

## Key questions

- What do you think this story is about?

- What makes you say that?

- Who do you think this is on the front cover?

- What are you going to write first?

- How does your story start?

- What happens next?

- How does your story end?

- Where are you going to write your name?

- What is the first sound you can hear at the beginning of the word?

- What sound comes next?

## Look, listen and note

- Note the children's emergent writing skills, the marks or letters they use to represent their name or objects.

- Note children's preferences in terms of the tools they choose to write with: pen, pencil, felt-tip pen, chalk, for example.

## Effective practice

- Always model correct formation of letters with the children.

- Encourage children to practise letter shapes.

- Give them opportunities to experiment away from paper – in the wet sand, in shaving foam, in paint, for example. Use builder's trays to contain the different media you are using.

## Planning and resourcing

- Always include writing opportunities in the role-play area.

- Ensure your writing area is always well stocked, looks inviting and provides a variety of writing opportunities such as letter-writing, filling in forms, book-making materials, notepads for shopping lists and diaries for appointments. Keep pencils and colouring pencils sharpened. Think about writing opportunities for the outdoor area as well, such as a role-play post office, a garden centre, or a builders' office on a building site.

## Home links

- Ensure that parents and carers are aware of the setting's handwriting policy.

- Give parents and carers a copy of correct letter formation so that they can support their children at home.

## Additional resources

### A selection of traditional tales

Look for the 'First Favourite Tales' series published by Penguin Books Ltd which retell traditional tales using rhythmic text.

- *The Princess and the Pea,* London: Ladybird. Simplified version of the classic tale. Part of the 'Read it Yourself' series.

- Cartwright, Stephen and Avery, Heather (2004) *The Usborne Book of Fairy Tales,* London: Usborne Publishing. Six classic fairy tales ('Cinderella', 'The Story of Rumpelstiltskin', 'Little Red Riding Hood', 'Sleeping Beauty', 'Goldilocks and the Three Bears' and 'The Three Little Pigs') are retold using dual-level text. On each page there is a simple line for beginner readers and a more complex one for those more advanced.

To support practice in correct letter formation, create alphabet books with the children. (For a selection of alphabet books see Additional Resources in Chapter 3 for the age group 'From 30–60 months'). Creating their own alphabet books will provide an opportunity for children to develop their early spelling skills using their phonic knowledge and will create a constructive link between reading and writing for beginner readers and writers. In relation to reading, children need to learn that phonemes should be blended, in order, from left to right, from the beginning of a word through to the end and in relation to writing, that words can be segmented into their constituent phonemes for spelling. Segmenting phonemes is the reverse of blending phonemes to read words (refer back to Section 2 of the theory section in this book for further clarification).

## An alternative story title

Ahlberg, Janet and Ahlberg, Allan (1999) *The Jolly Postman,* London: Puffin Books. The classic tale of the Jolly Postman's journey delivering post to fairy-tale characters. This is a great book for modelling the conventions of different genres of meaningful written communication including invitations, postcards and information leaflets. The possibilities are endless in supporting children to practise purposeful writing in real life situations.

# The EYFS principles

The above activities are designed to further support children as individuals on their own unique journey into conventional writing and handwriting. The activities do not put pressure on children to achieve landmarks by a certain time; they show, through the creation of enabling environments, how to monitor and respond to children developing hand–eye coordination and fine motor skills. The development of such skills will support children as they gradually move from meaningful mark making into conventional letter formation.

# Key technical vocabulary

**blend** The process of combining phonemes into larger elements such as clusters, syllables and words. Also refers to a combination of two or more phonemes, particularly at the beginning and end of words: 'st', 'str', 'nt', 'cl', 'ng'.

**compound word** A word made up of two other words, e.g., football, classroom, broomstick.

**digraph** Two letters representing one phoneme: 'ba_th_', 'tr_ai_n', 'ch/ur/ch'.

**split digraph**, e.g., make.

**grapheme** Written representation of a sound. There are 140 graphemes in the English language. Graphemes consist of one or more letters, e.g., 't', 'th', 'tch'.

**letter string** A group of letters which together represent a phoneme or morpheme.

**morpheme** The smallest unit of meaning. A word may consist of one morpheme ('house'), two morphemes ('house'/'s'), or three or more morphemes ('house'/'keep'/'ing'). Suffixes and prefixes are morphemes.

**onset** The initial consonant or consonant cluster of a word or syllable: 'clang', 'trike', 'sun'. Some words have no onset, e.g., 'or', 'use', 'out'.

**phoneme** The smallest unit of pronounceable sound in a word. There are approximately forty-four phonemes in English. A phoneme may be represented by one, two, three or four letters: to, shoe, through.

**prefix** A morpheme which can be added to the beginning of a word to change its meaning: in-finite, in-conclusive, in-edible.

**rhyme** Words containing the same rime in their final syllable are said to rhyme: 'acrobat', 'chat', 'down', 'clown'.

**rime** That part of a syllable which contains the vowel and final consonant or consonant cluster if there is one: 'at' in 'cat', 'orn' in 'horn', 'ow' in 'cow'. Some words consist of rime only: 'or', 'ate', 'eel'.

**root word** A word to which prefixes and suffixes may be added to make other words, e.g., in 'unclear', 'clearly', 'cleared', the root word is 'clear'.

**semantics** Awareness that a sentence or phrase makes sense within the text as a whole. Allows for predictive strategies.

**suffix** A morpheme which is added to the end of a word, e.g., 'head-ing'.

**syllable** Each beat in a word is a syllable. Words with only one beat are called monosyllabic, e.g., 'cat', 'fright', 'jail'. Words with more than one beat are called polysyllabic, e.g., 'super', 'coward', 'superficially'.

**syntax** The grammatical relationship between words, phrases and clauses, i.e. words and word order.

# References

Barrat-Pugh, C. (2002) 'Children as Writers', in L. Makin and C. Jones-Diaz (eds), *Literacies in Early Childhood: Challenging Views Challenging Practice,* Sydney: Maclennan & Petty.

Bearne, E. (1998) *Making Progress in English,* London: Routledge.

Bloodgood, J. (1999) 'What's in a Name? Children's Name Writing and Literacy Acquisition', *Reading Research Quarterly,* 34 (3): 342–67.

Bromley, H. (2006) *Making My Own Mark: Play and Writing,* London: Early Education.

Brooker, L. (2002) ' "Five on the First of December!" What Can We Learn from Case Studies of Early Childhood Literacy?' *Journal of Early Childhood Literacy,* 2 (3): 291–313.

Bruner, J. S. (1983) *Child's Talk: Learning to Use Language,* Oxford: Oxford University Press.

Chaplain, R. (2003) *Teaching Without Disruption in the Primary School,* London: RoutledgeFalmer.

Clay, M. M. (1975) *What Did I Write? Beginning Writing Behaviour,* Portsmouth, NH: Heinemann Educational Books.

—— (1993) *An Observation Survey or Early Literacy Achievement,* Hong Kong: Heinemann Education.

Collins, F. M. and Svensson, C. (2008) 'If I Had a Magic Wand I'd Magic Her Out of the Book: the Rich Literacy Practices of Competent Early Readers', *Early Years,* 28 (1): 81–91.

Compton-Lilly, C. (2006) 'Identity, Childhood Culture, and Literacy Learning: a Case Study', *Journal of Early Childhood Literacy,* 6 (1): 57–76.

Department for Education and Skills (DfES) (2007a) *The Early Years Foundation Stage,* Nottingham: DfES Publications.

—— (2007b) *Practice Guidance for the Early Years Foundation Stage,* Nottingham: DfES Publications.

—— (DfES) (2007c) *Letters and Sounds: Principles and Practice of High Quality Phonics,* Norwich: DfES Publications.

Dunsmuir, S., and Blatchford, P. (2004) 'Predictors of Writing Competence in 4- to 7-Year Old Children', *British Journal of Educational Psychology,* 74 (483): 461–83.

Dyson, A. (2001) 'Writing and Children's Symbolic Repertoires: Development Unhinged', in S. B. Neuman and D. K. Dickinson (eds), *Handbook of Early Literacy Research,* New York: The Guilford Press.

Ferreiro, E., and Teberosky, A. (1982) *Literacy Before Schooling,* Portsmouth, NH: Heinemann.

Gee, J. P. (2001) 'A Sociocultural Perspective in Early Literacy Development', in S. B. Neuman and D. K. Dickinson (eds), *Handbook of Early Literacy Research,* New York: The Guilford Press.

Gillen, J. and Hall, N. (2003) 'The Emergence of Early Childhood Literacy', in N. Hall, J. Larson, and J. Marsh (eds), *Handbook of Early Childhood Literacy,* London: Sage.

Goodman, Y. (1986) 'Readers' and Writers' Talk About Language', in C. Pontecorvo, B. Burge and L. B. Resnic (eds), *Children's Early Text Construction,* Upper Saddle River, NJ: Lawrence Erlbaum Associates.

Goswami, U. and Bryant, P. (1990) *Phonological Skills and Learning to Read,* London: Lawrence Erlbaum Associates.

Gregory, E. (2001) 'Sisters and Brothers as Language and Literacy Teachers: Synergy Between Siblings Playing and Working Together', *Journal of Early Childhood Literacy,* 1 (3): 301–22.

Hall, N. (1987) *The Emergence of Literacy,* London: Hodder and Stoughton.

Hall, N. and Robinson, A. (2003) *Exploring Play and Writing in the Early Years,* London: David Fulton.

Hannon, P., Weinberger, J. and Nutbrown, C. (1991) 'A Study of Work with Parents and Carers to Promote Early Literacy Development', *Research Papers in Education* 6 (2): 77–97.

Harste, J. C., Woodward, V. A., and Burke, C. L. (1984) *Language Stories and Literacy Lessons,* Portsmouth, NH: Heinemann Educational Books.

Heath, S. E. (1983) *Ways with Words: Language, Life and Work in Communities and Classrooms,* Cambridge: Cambridge University Press.

Kirkpatrick, A. (2001) 'Preschool Writing Development and the Role of Parents and Carers', in C. Nutbrown (ed.), *Research Studies in Early Childhood Education,* London: Trentham Books.

Kress, G. (1996) *Before Writing: Rethinking the Paths to Literacy,* London: Routledge.

Lancaster, L. (2003) 'Moving into Literacy: How It All Begins', in N. Hall, J. Larson and J. Marsh (eds), *Handbook of Early Childhood Literacy,* London: Sage.

Martello, J. (2001) 'Talk About Writing: Metalinguistic Awareness in Beginning Writers', *Australian Journal of Language and Literacy,* 24 (2): 101–11.

—— (2002) 'Many Roads Through Many Modes: Becoming Literate in Early Childhood', in L. Makin and C. Jones-Diaz (eds), *Literacies in Early Childhood Challenging Views: Challenging Practice,* Sydney: Maclennan & Petty.

—— (2004) 'Precompetence and Trying to Learn: Beginning Writers Talk About Spelling', *Journal of Early Childhood Literacy,* 4 (3): 271–89.

McMullen, M. B. and Darling, C. A. (2003) 'Learning from Their Mistakes: Glimpses of Symbolic Functioning in Two-and-a-Half to Three-Year Old Children', *Early Years,* 23 (1): 55–66.

Meek, M. (1991) *On Being Literate,* London: The Bodley Head.

Mehrabian, A. (1971) *Silent Messages,* Belmont, Calif.: Wadsworth.

Messer, D. (2006) 'Current Perspectives on Language Acquisition', in J. S. Peccei (ed.), *Child Language: a Resource Book for Students,* London: Routledge.

Miller, L., and Smith, A. P. (2004) 'Practitioners' Beliefs and Children's Experiences of Literacy in Four Early Years Settings', *Early Years* 24 (2): 121–33.

Neuman, S. B., and Dickinson, D. K. (eds) (2001) *Handbook of Early Literacy Research,* New York: The Guilford Press.

Neuman, S. B. and Roskos, K. (1997) 'Literacy Knowledge in Practice: Contexts of Participation in Young Writers and Readers', *Reading Research Quarterly* 32 (1): 10–32.

Nowicki, S. and Duke, M. (2000) *Helping the Child Who Doesn't Fit In,* Atlanta, Ga.: Peachtree.

Nutbrown, C. and Hannon, P. (2003) 'Children's Perceptions on Family Literacy: Methodological Issues, Findings and Implications for Practice', *Journal of Early Childhood Literacy* 3 (2): 115–45.

Pahl, K. (1999) *Transformations: Meaning Making in a Nursery*, London: Trentham.

Pellegrini, A. D. (2001) 'Some Theoretical and Methodological Considerations in Studying Literacy in Social Context', in S. B. Neuman and D. K. Dickinson (eds), *Handbook of Early Literacy Research,* New York: The Guilford Press.

Peccei, J. S. (2006) *Child Language: A Resource Book for Students,* London: Routledge.

Purcell-Gates, V. (1986) 'Stories, Coupons, and the TV Guide: Relationships Between Home Literacy Experiences and Emergent Literacy Knowledge', *Reading Research Quarterly,* 31 (4): 406–28.

Rowe, D. W. (1994) *Preschoolers as Authors: Literacy Learning in the Social World of the Classroom,* Cresskill, NJ: Hampton Press.

—— (2003) 'The Nature of Young Children's Authoring', in N. Hall, J. Larson, and J. Marsh (eds), *Handbook of Early Childhood Literacy,* London: Sage.

Shankweiler, D. and Fowler, A. E. (2004) 'Questions People Ask About the Role of Phonological Process in Learning to Read', *Reading and Writing: An Interdisciplinary Journal,* 17: 483–515.

Siraj-Blatchford, I. and Clarke, P. (2000) *Supporting Identity, Diversity and Language in the Early Years,* Buckingham: Open University Press.

Teale, W. and Sulzby, E. (1986) *Emergent Literacy: Writing and Reading,* Norwood, NJ: Ablex.

Tizard, B. and Hughes, M. (1984) *Young Children Learning,* London: Fontana.

Vygotsky, L. (1978) *Mind in Society: The Development of Higher Psychological Processes,* Cambridge, Mass.: Harvard University Press.

—— (1986) *Thought and Language,* Cambridge, Mass.: MIT Press.

Wells, G. (1986) *The Meaning Makers: Children Learning Language and Using Language to Learn,* London: Hodder and Stoughton.

Whitehead, M. (2002) *Language and Literacy with Young Children,* London: Paul Chapman.

Wray, D. (1994) *Literacy and Awareness,* London: Hodder and Stoughton.

Wray, D., Bloom, W. and Hall, N. (1989) *Literacy in Action,* Barcombe: Falmer.

Yang, H. C. and Noel, A. M. (2006) 'The Developmental Characteristics of Four- and Five-Year-Old Pre-Schoolers' Drawings: An Analysis of Scribbles, Placement Patterns, Emergent Writing, and Name Writing in Archived Spontaneous Drawing Samples', *Journal of Early Childhood Literacy,* 6 (2): 145–62.

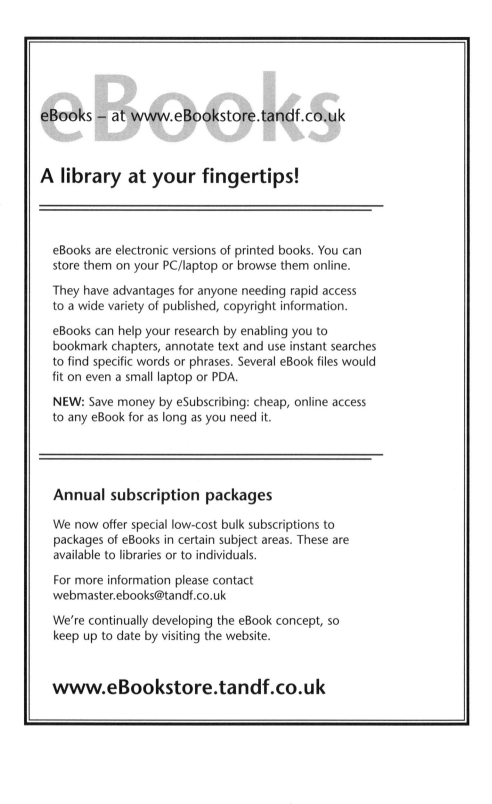